Praise for *The 7 Non-Negotiables of Winning*

"David Williams is a great leader and friend. He has a leadership style that provides just the right mix of guidance and empowerment. David carefully prioritizes his stewardships, crafting success with meticulous care and determination. We have the privilege of working with David and appreciate his fierce dedication and fire. He has a knack for discovering diamonds in the rough and molding them into amazing leaders. We are honored to endorse and contribute to this book in support of our great CEO. We commit to be in the arena together every day to help one another and businesses to soar."

—Team Fishbowl

"The minute you step into the Fishbowl office, you feel something very different. And now I know what it is we felt: Respect, Belief, Trust, Loyalty, Commitment, Courage, and Gratitude. Everyone we met that day exuded *The 7 Non-Negotiables of Winning*. So it's no wonder Fishbowl is as wildly successful as it is."

—Ed Bagley
Director, Communications, O.C. Tanner Company

"Fishbowl is an outstanding member of the community, that Zion is pleased to support. They not only care about their employees and customers—but their concern and compassion extends to everyone. I thank them for standing strong for businesses by sharing *The 7 Non-Negotiables of Winning*. There is no downside to Respect, Belief, Trust, Loyalty, Commitment, Courage, and Gratitude."

—Brad Adamson
Senior Vice President, Zions Bank

"I found David's book a treasure trove of not only things to avoid in building your business career but things to proactively DO. David's *The 7 Non-Negotiables of Winning* and his personal commitment to practice them have clearly led to a fantastic outcome for Fishbowl and its employees, partners, and customers—and I am confident there a many more good things to come for all involved. I think that David's book should be required reading for all businesspeople, but especially small business entrepreneurs."

—Randy Pierson
CEO, Strategic Solution Advisors, LLC

"To be 'inside the Bowl' is the best kind of culture shock—an experience in camaraderie, zeal, professional hospitality, and joy. I believe *The 7 Non-Negotiables of Winning* are the basis of this incredible and highly productive culture Fishbowl enjoys—a positive philosophy that impacts its employees, partners, and customers in powerful ways. It is truly refreshing."

—Joe Woodard
Chief Executive Officer, The Woodard Consulting Group

"In *The 7 Non-Negotiables of Winning*, David and the entire Fishbowl team prove that there are intrinsic, time-tested ways to live and lead rooted in traits that will inevitably create personal and organizational growth. As a 'friend of the Bowl,' I've observed the non-negotiables in action from close range and have nothing but admiration for the culture of investment and growth that Fishbowl has created. The 7 Non-Negotiables are real, and they fuel real growth."

—Rob Moore
Vice President Client Services, Certiport, Pearson Vue

"There are truly some things in life that are non-negotiable; David Williams has laid that out in convincing language. We are proud to be a Fishbowl partner and look forward to continuing our wonderful relationship."

—Sal Cucinella
Chief Executive Officer, Sharpe Concepts

"*The 7 Non-Negotiables of Winning* brings together many practical ideas one should consider when looking at organizational design and the interaction of a team. Building trust, showing loyalty and commitment, and highlighting the achievement of others through gratitude are all elements a great leader needs to master. This book reminds us that our personal interactions with those around us can turn something ordinary into something great. We must encourage and promote what is possible. It is only through these positive interactions with others that difficult and great things can be accomplished."

—Jim Holm
Executive Vice President, Certiport, Pearson Vue

"David's book reinforces the need for all of us to treat others as we would like to be treated. Through relevant storytelling he is able to weave the importance of honesty and integrity into personal conduct. In seldom seen fashion this book will help one self-evaluate both business and personal behavior and encourage positive changes."

—Matt Peterson
President and CEO, EFileCabinet

"A must-read book for executives and managers trying to get the best from and for their employees. This is a poignant and powerful collection of insights from one of the great business and people leaders on what it takes to become a better CEO, manager, employee, father, or friend."

—Peter Wride
Director of Operations, Ascent Advisor

"*The 7 Non-Negotiables of Winning* came to life for me when I visited Fishbowl while writing an article for *Forbes*. Everything I encountered at the company was different. Employees weren't just happy, they were empowered. The power of the principles is clear: nothing less than your happiness and success in life and career depend on mastering the 7 Non-Negotiables."

—Devin Thorpe
Champion of Social Good; Author of *Your Mark on the World*

"Whether you are starting a company or an executive of a Fortune 100 company, David walks you through the 7 Non-Negotiables that will help you build a lasting company that cultivates world-class talent and achieves extraordinary results."

—Burke Alder
Vice President of Marketing, Lendio

"Fishbowl is on FIRE in a very good way! Their socially conscious style of corporate responsibility is blazing a trail for other entrepreneurs to follow. The Fishbowl flame of success burns brightly. *The 7 Non-Negotiables of Winning* is inspiring!"

—Anne R. Wairepo, PhD
Director, Utah Valley University, Women's Success Center

"There are very few people who celebrate their people and the accomplishments of their people. After visiting Fishbowl, getting to know their people and then reading this book, I can say most confidently that this is the written version of how their company family lives, values, works, and achieves. As you turn the pages you will feel that each non-negotiable is a core value that should be implemented immediately within your own life, workplace, and goals.

—Leialoha Pakalani
Assistant Director/Career Counselor, Woodbury School of
Business/MBA, Utah Valley University

"David is an inspiration and an example to everyone he comes in contact with. I can count many, many lessons from the 7 Non-Negotiables (such as 'Fail Up') that I now carry with me and that will continue to influence my decisions and future."

—Cheryl Snapp Conner
Managing Partner, Snapp Conner PR

"I love *The 7 Non-Negotiables of Winning*! In this ever-changing world it is great to see David and Mary solidly founded on timeless principles! I have seen the inside workings of Fishbowl and can attest to the joy that is found inside the Bowl!"

—Mike Lewis
EVP Sales, AirComUSA/FaxPipe

"I have had many different experiences where I have seen the David and the Fishbowl family live these proven principles as they have run their business and it has had a profound effect on all that come in contact with them. As a friend and partner, it is great to associate with individuals that not only preach such practices, but live them every day."

—Ben Bush
President, Voonami, Inc.

"It is often a rare event and a privilege during your career or life that you come across individuals such as David Williams and the Fishbowl team. Their unwavering belief in their team and how to apply the principles of Respect, Belief, Trust, Loyalty, Commitment, Courage, and Gratitude in this book are a true inspiration to all. This is something we should all strive for every day."

—Simon Jupe
Managing Director, Fishbowl Australia/Fishbowl New Zealand

"Fishbowl is a wonderful and unique business built on principles of integrity and high moral values. It is refreshing to see these principles that are often talked about (and not lived) actually applied by a company."

—James M. Martinos
President/CEO, Elite IT Partners, Inc.

"*The 7 Non-Negotiables of Winning* will change the face of work across the globe and I am pleased to support and endorse this book."

—John D. Cuny
President, World Class Health Enterprises

"The exemplary culture that David has meticulously crafted at Fishbowl, where every individual is valued as a leader embodying the 7 Non-Negotiables of Winning, is a smart blueprint for 21st century companies. Fishbowl is clear proof that companies that truly care about people and actively engage in strengthening their local and global communities through authentic values will not only achieve enduring success and a meaningful legacy, but they will also make the journey an enjoyable adventure for all involved."

—David Saedi
Chief Executive Officer, Ducasse Education

"Without hesitation, I can say that David is 'one in a million!' From his leadership to his modeling of good management and coaching skills there are few who do it better. The culture that he has carefully and deliberately created at Fishbowl is most refreshing and unique in corporate America! I am honored to associate with people of David's caliber."

—Jerry Johnson
Senior Training Consultant, InsideOut Development

The 7

NON-NEGOTIABLES
OF WINNING

The 7

NON-NEGOTIABLES
OF WINNING
Tying Soft Traits to Hard Results

David K. Williams

WILEY

Published by John Wiley & Sons, Inc., Hoboken, New Jersey.
Published simultaneously in Canada.

For general information about our other products and services, please contact our Customer
Care Department within the United States at (800) 762-2974, outside the United States at
(317) 572-3993 or fax (317) 572-4002.

Wiley publishes in a variety of print and electronic formats and by print-on-demand.
Some material included with standard print versions of this book may not be included in
e-books or in print-on-demand. If this book refers to media such as a CD or DVD that
is not included in the version you purchased, you may download this material at http://
booksupport.wiley.com. For more information about Wiley products, visit www.wiley.com.

Library of Congress Cataloging-in-Publication Data:

Williams, David K., 1958–
    The 7 Non-Negotiables of Winning: Tying Soft Traits to Hard Results / David K. Williams.
       pages cm
    Includes index.
    ISBN: 978-1-118-57164-4 (cloth); ISBN: 978-1-118-73920-4 (ebk);
    ISBN: 978-1-118-73940-2 (ebk)
       1. Interpersonal relations.   2. Respect.   3. Success.   4. Employee motivation.
    I. Title.   II. Title: Seven non-negotiables of winning.
    HM1106.W555   2013
    302—dc23

                                                                        2013016034

Printed in the United States of America
10 9 8 7 6 5 4 3 2 1

It is not the critic who counts;

not the man who points out how the strong man stumbled

or

where the doer of deeds could have done them better.

The credit belongs to the man who is actually in the arena,

whose face is marred by dust and sweat and blood; who strives valiantly;

who errs and comes short again and again; who knows great enthusiasms,

the great devotions;

who spends himself in a worthy cause;

who at the best,

knows in the end the triumph of high achievement,

and who, at the worst,

if he fails, at least fails while daring greatly

so that his place shall never be with those timid souls who

know neither victory nor defeat.

—Theodore Roosevelt

I dedicate this book to my wife, Paula, and my son, Cameron Williams, who inspire us to keep the flame of all that is noble and courageous burning strong.

Williams Family.
Left to right: David Bauerle and grandson Corbin, Amber, David, Paula, Cameron, Charisse, Tanner, and Lindsey

This photo was taken a couple of weeks after we found out that Cam had cancer. Throughout his journey he remained steadfast in his faith and optimism. He never doubted, wavered, complained, or asked why.

I also dedicate this book to our company, Fishbowl—where our people manifest the principles and outcomes described in this book by trying a little bit harder each day to be a little bit better.

CONTENTS

FOREWORD

Brad Smith, Intuit president and CEO, is a longtime Fishbowl friend and partner who mirrors our commitment to being in the people business. Even as the leader of a billion-dollar corporation, Brad is so down to earth that he never forgets that people from all walks of life can be equal partners if their Soft Traits are aligned.

I first met David in the gym, not in the boardroom. We had recently accepted new roles in our respective organizations and were in search of the best ideas and inspiration to guide us on our new journeys. You can call our chance meeting serendipity or luck, but many years later, we simply call each other friends.

His visible intensity and search for excellence were the traits that originally caught my eye, but it was his humanity and willingness to give of himself that touched my heart. A champion is never measured by the number of times they hit the canvas, but whether they have the strength of will to get up and continue the contest.

David always stands up and does so with such dignity and grace that he serves as an inspiration to all around him. I count myself among those blessed individuals who have become better versions of themselves because they have known David Williams.

—Brad Smith
President and Chief Executive Officer, Intuit

PREFACE

Y ou don't have to be a CEO to find this book useful. I wrote it for leaders, midlevel employees, students, homemakers, and anyone else who has goals and wants to do something great with their lives. I will show you that it's okay to fail as long as you keep your eye on the end goal and follow seven basic principles I use every day in my business: the 7 Non-Negotiables.

I believe in people, not just their output. When leaders trust their employees and give them creative freedom to try new things, they consistently achieve positive results in the long run. This book is for individuals who don't feel like they fit the standard corporate mold, in which a person's worth is measured on a scale of 1 to 10 and money is the sole driving force of the business.

In this book, I share what we developed as a team as we built a successful company and, far more important, a place where people could enjoy working together in collaboration. There is no perfect work methodology, just as there is no perfect employee. We are all evolving and growing together. We are far from perfect and we embrace our failures as opportunities to learn. I have lived, learned, and strived to do better each day, and that is all that I can ask of everyone in the Bowl.

Early in my career, I was lucky enough to have patient leaders who saw past my youthful errors to realize what I was capable of. As a result, I was able to do and be better. They provided me with opportunities to develop and grow, and this has helped me accomplish extraordinary things that I didn't even realize I could do. It's therefore only right that now, as a CEO, I return the favor to my own employees and strive to educate others about a simple truth

I learned long ago: The secret to success is to *Fail Up* and move forward.

The key to Failing Up is to connect Soft Traits to Hard Results. You can continuously benefit from Hard Results—those that you can measure and quantify, and that show a return on investment—as you add to and strengthen your Soft Traits—your characteristics and attributes. When we see our Hard Results in action, we naturally become more motivated to increase and improve our Soft Traits. Likewise, we will naturally see growth in our Hard Results as we increase the competency and capacity of our Soft Traits.

> Learn from the mistakes of others. You can't live long enough to make them all yourself.
>
> —*Eleanor Roosevelt*

An example of a Soft Trait in action: No matter how hard you try, you are going to make some mistakes. While the fear of failing has the effect of immobilizing us, you will find new freedom in accepting your failures as opportunities to learn and develop in new ways. You do not have to accept the judgment of others about your successes or shortcomings. Their perspective is part of their learning path—not yours. What matters most is how you respond to your mistakes. If you accept accountability, grow, and move forward and upward, you can achieve great things. Some of the greatest triumphs in history took place right after, and can be tied directly to, the biggest failures.

ACKNOWLEDGMENTS

In the end, everyone will know that everyone did it.

—Lao Tzu

No worthwhile journey is ever embarked upon alone. This book is the culmination of a lifetime of shared learning, failures, and successes. The concepts presented are universal, yet the experiences shared are my personal life lessons and Fishbowl's. This book wrote itself through our shared experiences at Fishbowl. There is a bit of DNA from every single Fishbowler who currently swims in the Bowl in this book.

My heartfelt thanks goes out to everyone who helped create this meaningful journey that has no ending.

To my Fishbowl Family, who works hard each day to bring these stories to life; my personal family, for their love, understanding, and support; Mary Michelle Scott, my business partner, who assisted in compiling the contents and who partners with me to lead our company and Courage Above Mountains initiatives; our Fishbowl Captains, John David King, Dusty Miller, John Erickson, Kirk Tanner, Kevin Batchelor, and Heber Billings; and Rick Weiss, for lending his talents in creating the great cover artwork.

A special thank you to our Fishbowlers, who show up every day and bring the Bowl to life with positive energy and an extraordinary exuberance for living. They make it all worthwhile. And to all our U.S. Fishbowl partners, including Intuit CEO Brad Smith, and

Fishbowl Australia's Simon Jupe, who keep things moving forward with an ocean of support.

My appreciation to everyone who participated in creating the *Forbes* columns: Cheryl Snapp Conner of Snapp Conner PR; *Forbes* Managing Editor Tom Post; and Robert Lockard, our amazing Fishbowl Copy Editor; those who contributed on social media; and the countless others who have contributed in ways known and unknown.

INTRODUCTION

Entrepreneur by Choice

When anyone calls Fishbowl asking to invest in our company, I always respond, with sincerity and on behalf of our team, "We are employee owned, debt free, we grow with our own cash, and our exit strategy is death. We probably don't fit your investment model."

Most investors are taken aback by my response because in their world everything has a price. But my world works differently. Some things are not for sale and cannot be bought—and Fishbowl is one of them. I value how our employees feel about our company more than the price potential investors would pay for it or what I might personally gain. I understand why in the business world we call venture capital money "funding." Starting your business $1 million to $10 million in debt never appealed to me or the team at Fishbowl. When we need funds, we earn them, or we work with local banks to secure loans that can be quickly paid back.

We have publicly stated that we will never sell Fishbowl, go public, or adopt a mainstream corporate mentality. Fishbowl belongs to current and future generations of Fishbowlers—and always will. In 2012, 50 employees became co-owners of the company, and in 2013 we added an additional 21 who successfully and consistently demonstrated the 7 Non-Negotiables. This book is about our journey, our lessons learned, our achievements, and our Fail Ups.

LAYING THE FOUNDATION FOR SUCCESS: THE RHYTHM OF BUSINESS IN THE BOWL

I have been an entrepreneur from my earliest recollection. I never wanted to be anything else. I had a dream of what I thought could be the greatest company in the world to work for; yet for some reason, I never thought that dream would ever become reality. Somehow that company came to be—and I had a hand in making it happen. Today I am the CEO of a fast-growing business of approximately 100 individuals in Orem, Utah, that makes award-winning inventory management software. Our product, Fishbowl Inventory, is the number one requested inventory software for use with QuickBooks for business. Many Fortune 500 companies also use Fishbowl Inventory as a stand-alone asset tracking tool.

Our work will never be easy—and that's the way we like it in the Bowl. We love a good challenge. Our company is located at the base of Mount Timpanogos, which is the heart of one of the most breathtaking mountain ranges in Utah. While it's a magnificent mountain, it's not an easy climb—and that's why it's crucial for us to have the company right there. It serves as a reminder to always look up, and remain open and optimistic. We like to break a sweat and work hard as we climb higher. We also relish playing, laughing, and exploring along the way.

Did I choose to be an entrepreneur or did I simply fall into the Bowl?

I consider myself an entrepreneur by choice. My path into entrepreneurship was set long ago. The following are a few of the qualities that define me, as well as most of my colleagues at Fishbowl:

1. *No business title will ever fit for long.* We are like fish, which must keep swimming to stay vibrant and alive. As such, our teams change functions and offices multiple times per year.

2. *Leaders aren't necessarily appointed.* Rather, they emerge naturally to fill specific needs. Fish swim better in schools.

3. *We will never embrace a corporate mentality.* We dislike being bossed around, yet we will give it our all for the team and for

one another. Fish instinctively know how to swim and in which direction to travel. Our overriding policy is: Don't tap on the glass! In other words, we don't work well when stress is used to force an outcome. We prefer calm water, yet we can weather even the most treacherous storms if necessary.

4. *We love to build things, to play together, and to help people.* Give us a challenging project that supports the greater good, then give us enough space and time, and we will consistently exceed expectations.

5. *Our work must be noble and for something larger than ourselves* because we are in the *people* business. Our customers and partners are our friends. We show up at work each day to see people we are excited to spend time with. Happy fish create great products and happy customers. This is what contributes to significant growth in revenue year after year more than any other factor. And even more important than the revenue is the remarkable journey to success.

6. *We are both fiercely independent workers and extraordinary team players.* On the surface, this sounds like a contradiction in terms, but it is what makes Fishbowl remarkable. The 7 Non-Negotiables make it possible for us to perform as individual champions and also to build one of the greatest companies in the history of inventory management software and solutions. No one sits on the bench on Team Fishbowl.

The Value of Personal Development

Every activity I start I pursue with my whole heart, all out. I have no middle ground. "I'll quit competing when my heart quits beating," said Michael Jordan, and I concur. I love sports and activities where I compete on my own and as a team. I play the piano. I ran a marathon. I am constantly competing against myself and working to break my own records. I swam over a mile every morning for several years and then moved on to road biking, averaging more than 100 miles per week. And 15 years ago, I started bodybuilding—a form of exercise and self-expression I continue to engage in to this day. I didn't just lift weights; I competed until I had won the top natural body-building competition award in the 20 Western States at the age of 50. From this experience, I learned a valuable lesson:

No activity that matters to you should be pursued only halfway.

As important as giving your all is, avoiding burnout is equally essential. I set a pace and rhythm for winning the big prize, yet I still employ my intense natural laser focus to accomplish the goal. One hundred percent is the only option for me. If you are only 85 percent committed, then you are not committed. And this is true for *all* aspects of life.

In my personal life, I set the speed, temperature, and pace on extreme, yet I work in a calm, easy Bowl.

How does this work?

The first Non-Negotiable, Respect, empowers me to show up as my authentic self. It also empowers everyone else to bring his or her unique talents, gifts, and rhythm of work to Fishbowl.

Perhaps you are hoping to discover the secret to building a success-ful career, or find out the tips and tricks of the trade. I mentioned that I care about people and how to please them—so I'll let you in on one extremely important secret. Lesson 1 begins right here—and it starts with you: What you put out in the world returns to you in equal measure.

There are no shortcuts or quick fixes. It's your life. Make the most of every moment because you don't know how many of those moments you are going to get. My son, Cam, only lived 25 years on this earth, but he lived more in that short time than many who reach a ripe old age. He never wasted a minute. He is remembered today not for his work title but for how he loved and uplifted people. Every year on February 16 we celebrate Cam's life and legacy. In Chapter 6, I go into detail about Cam's celebration of life, his herculean battle to survive, and what we who knew him continue to learn from his example.

However long we live—and whether we realize it or not—we all leave something behind. Have you thought about what your legacy will be? How do you show up in the world of work each day? Many employees today like to keep their options open. They show up for work while keeping an updated résumé on the market and then wonder why nothing remarkable is happening for them in the workplace. Consider doing something different: Arrive at work and dedicate yourself like it's the last job you will ever have. After this, see whether your experience has been transformed. Respect the job you have and the people you work with—and if you find you cannot do this in your current position, dedicate yourself to finding one where you can and *will*.

One of the most important lessons I will share in this book is that every individual sets his or her own pace. The intensity that I set for myself reflects my personal goals. The 7 Non-Negotiables are the guiding principles at Fishbowl; they create a solid foundation so that everyone can develop and contribute their own unique gifts. They are the compass that helps us all to discover our "True North."

I share with you my personal experiences so you can learn from the mistakes I've made while enjoying the benefits of hindsight. There is a way to be extreme and laser-focused without sucking all the energy and life out of your teams. At Fishbowl, we call this "adjusting the trim tab." I believe that all people have the potential to be a trim tab, which is the small rudder that makes small adjustments to the big rudder that turns the entire ship. People just have to be willing to lead and cause a ripple effect through their influence, no matter what position they hold.

A leader doesn't need to leave a big wake to be effective or build a great company. A true leader acknowledges those who support him during the journey.

THE SINGLE GREATEST SECRET OF LEADERSHIP: FAILING UP

I am only an average man, but, by George, I work harder at it than the average man.

—*Theodore Roosevelt*

After years of constant struggle, banging my head against the wall of success and failure, I finally broke through to the far side of complexity and arrived at something I never expected to find: simplicity. I learned that achieving success doesn't have to be overly complicated.

This is the secret that led to the simple realization of the greatest trait that drives my success: I have learned to *Fail Up*.

It has taken much of my life to discover what I am *great* at. So when I fail, I fail big. I allowed my failures to define, limit, and even incapacitate me for many years. I was not open to the possibility that success is a journey. Failure is an integral and inevitable set of stops in the process, and I simply needed to get back on the right track.

When I finally discovered this secret—when I changed my paradigm—it changed my life. I no longer define others or myself as failures when we don't accomplish what we initially set out to do. Instead, I recognize and appreciate that there are areas in our lives we have mastered, areas we are developing, and areas where we haven't even scratched the surface yet.

As leaders, we serve our employees best by encouraging them to navigate through challenges on their journey. We can help by asking questions like "How do you learn best?" "What could you do better?" or "How can the team better support you in the future?"

The important thing is to move forward continually. Some days we make great progress in some areas; other days we seem to slide back a bit. If we were to chart our progress, it would have ups and downs, but overall it should move upward as we live and learn from our mistakes and failures. This is the heart of Failing Up.

There were times when my personal challenges brought me to my knees and broke me to the point I couldn't even get out of bed. I wanted to throw in the towel because I just didn't know what to do. I wanted to give up, but I didn't. I hope you won't have to fall as far as I did to learn how high you can bounce back.

We often struggle to see what we can learn from challenges because they seem unfair and impossible to bear while we're in them. I will never understand why I lost my son when he was only 25 years old and in the prime of his life. For a long time, I felt like I had failed because I could not find a way to help him get better. I also felt lost because I didn't know how to cope with his absence.

Even if we don't understand why bad things happen to us, we can Fail Up from them and become better people and build better businesses as a result. My own path hasn't been an easy journey by any means; but I no longer get lost in the weeds. I live, learn, and move forward.

My life is far from perfect. But I have learned that if you *haven't* experienced failure—or have ignored the lessons inherent in the process—you're missing out on your most invaluable opportunities for growth. Don't be afraid to fail—and don't waste energy trying to cover up failures. Learn from them, and move on to the next challenge. Learn to look for the "gold in them thar hills," take the gold from the experience, and leave the failure behind.

PEOPLE, PRIORITIES, AND PURPOSE

I want to change the world—not so that others will know I've changed the world, but because I feel a genuine desire to help people. I do my best to never quit or give up on anything or anyone. Admittedly, this has led to some disastrous results because I stayed in some positions far too long. Though it hurt me at the time, I have the blessing of perspective today as I look back on those experiences of standing steadfast and immovable. I realize now that these have been some of the most character-defining periods of my life, regardless of the financial gain or loss, or the perception of right or wrong.

I have made it a habit to think about people first and money second. I've made—and lost—a lot of money throughout my career. And while being financially successful is rewarding, losing a lot of money taught me that life goes on, and it has helped me see that I don't really need money to be happy. People, on the other hand, bring tremendous joy to my life. I love people. Relationships are what I cannot live without.

You (yes, you!) are the only person capable of putting up roadblocks that keep you from achieving what you want to be in business, as well as in life. I have come to believe that our challenges in life are placed there to serve an important purpose: to determine how serious we are about our choices.

The ability to look beyond the current circumstances to see the ultimate possibilities and eventual outcome is something that every great leader has within himself or herself. And it's also something that every aspiring leader must *absolutely* learn. It will make the greatest difference in his or her effectiveness, in his or her company's ability to succeed, and even in the success of his or her career and personal relationships. This means accepting that failure is inevitable. It also means cultivating the ability to continually Fail Up.

SETTING THE GROUNDWORK

In this book, I will teach the 7 Non-Negotiables, the seven basic principles I use every day in our business and in life. Some will come faster than others, but that's okay. You have your entire life ahead of you to continually work on these traits. All you need to do is improve yourself a little bit further each day, and to rejoice and even have fun in the process of celebrating what you've learned after every mistake. Here is a framework that will help you and your organization get started:

Creating the Fundamental Framework for Ongoing Growth and Development

1. The Organizational Ecosystem
2. Your Interpersonal Ecosystem
3. The Value of Employee Ownership
4. Creating Long-Term Trust: Full Disclosure of Financials and Key Performance Indicators (KPIs)

THE ORGANIZATIONAL ECOSYSTEM

We must, indeed, all hang together, or most assuredly we shall all hang separately.

—*Benjamin Franklin in the Continental Congress*
before he signed the Declaration of Independence in 1776

If we are not continually taking care of the weaker parts of the company, we will eventually pass away as a company. The whole of any organization is a sum of its parts. When parts are weakened, the whole is weakened, and it could eventually perish. Think about this in terms of business. When you give someone a performance review in which you highlight all the things that they did wrong, ask your-self: Did this weaken or strengthen the individual and, ultimately, the team and the whole organization? When we speak about others when they are not present, does this strengthen or weaken the team?

As I mentioned in the Preface, I wrote this book for leaders, mid-level employees, students, homemakers, and anyone else who has goals and who wants to do something meaningful with their life. I will show you that it's okay to fail as long as you keep your eye on the end goal and follow the 7 Non-Negotiables. I promise you that by reading, digesting, and then putting them into action through the fun processes, exercises, and games throughout the book, that you will improve in all of the Non-Negotiables. And as you improve in any of the 7 Non-Negotiables in one of your life roles, you will find that there is a cascading effect across other roles.

YOUR INTERPERSONAL ECOSYSTEM

It's important to note that rarely does anyone who is truly successful in business go it alone. One of the most important support roles in an entrepreneurial company is not the founder or owner—it's the role of that person's significant other, partner or spouse, and family members. This is a timeless principle.

There is a prevalent myth that being the spouse of an entrepreneur is highly desirable—that it's great to be married to someone who loves their work and is taking creative risks. That being your own boss leaves you with a greater income and the flexibility to take time off for vacations or to attend to family needs.

In actuality, the opposite is typically true. The truth of the entre-preneurial life is a tornado of long hours, high risk, and uncertainty. Despite their good intentions, entrepreneurs can be the world's worst spouses, since they are usually investing the majority of their time in their companies, even during prosperous times.

Prior to my opportunity at Fishbowl, my wife, Paula Williams, had ample experience with the highs and lows of being married to an all-or-nothing entrepreneur. We have been married for 33 years. While raising five children, Paula endured moving 20 times. A highly con-servative person by nature, she is married to someone who envisions himself as full-on warrior, and she has been steadfast in her devotion, whether the bacon was being brought home or not. She encouraged me to go and be myself.

Ten years ago I bet the farm on a massive land reclamation deal. After three years of investing everything we had, one day it suddenly folded. Everyone jumped ship and I was the last man standing. I anguished and sought counsel over what to do. Should I declare bankruptcy? Not knowing if the house would be lost or the utilities shut off would lead most spouses and children to complain and act fearfully. Not mine. My family remained steadfast in cheering me on. By contrast, we had a close friend who forced his way into the business venture with additional investment money, and when the deal went south, he left threatening messages on our phone and wrote letters to my children telling them what a loser of a father they had.

Three years later, we had survived the process of repaying more than $1 million in debt. We paid off 72 credit cards without missing a payment. The leases and everything else we owed were all paid off. At any time, if the negative pressure I faced had come from within my home, I likely would have foregone my entrepreneurial life and chosen a different path. But because of Paula's patience (and because the creditors had been willing to work with me, thankfully), I was able to avoid bankruptcy and to remain standing when the opportunity to lead Fishbowl came along.

Likewise, without the strength of our Fishbowl family, we would have been unable to endure losing our oldest son, Cam, to a rare cancer just four years ago. The trials we face can either make us or break us. When the challenges have nearly broken me as an entrepreneur, my wife and family have remained strong.

I'd like to issue a challenge to every entrepreneur who has the support of a steadfast spouse or a significant other: Don't ever forget that your ability to be who you are and accomplish business miracles is equally dependent on them. Let us always appreciate, respect, and reward the vital roles that they play in our ability to reach entrepreneurial goals. Let us always make time in our lives to respect and support their dreams and endeavors. For example, Paula is now a member of the Mormon Tabernacle Choir, and I love being in the audience supporting and cheering her on, just as she has always done for me.

The Value of Employee Ownership

If business owners want to achieve unsurpassed output and generosity of spirit from employees, they need to share the pie with them. It is only through ownership that an individual ultimately dedicates his or her full mind and heart to the workplace. Our employees appreciate that they are helping to build a company that will endure the test of time. They take this stewardship seriously. Compare this with the feelings of an employee who is working to build a company that will ultimately be sold off.

At Fishbowl, we are committed to being employee-owned. There are currently 71 owners of Fishbowl with a piece of the company. We give stock solely on how employees are progressing in the 7 Non-Negotiables. No one is perfect in any of them, but the constant improvement and focus on them is paramount. We don't give stock options out on any other basis. Not tenure, role, or output. It's all about becoming a better person, a better teammate, a better servant leader.

Using the 7 Non-Negotiables in this way has been nothing short of miraculous: We are helping employees focus on what makes them better people, not only here at work but also in all the roles of their lives. Everyone manifests the 7 Non-Negotiables in unique ways, but everyone needs to be unified in trying a little bit harder each day to do a little bit better.

We have a 100-year-and-beyond plan at Fishbowl. We will be long gone in 100 years, but we are confident that the guiding principles outlined in this book will live on.

Creating Long-Term Trust: Full Disclosure of Financials and KPIs

To demonstrate how highly we value trust at Fishbowl as a business and personal attribute, we share financials with all employees the day they walk in. Given that part of their compensation is commission based, it is only fair for them to see that, beyond focusing on the revenue side, we are also fiscally minded. There is nothing like being out of debt. The freedom we have of not needing to march to the beat of an outside investor or bank is beautiful beyond words.

To preserve this independence, we grow with our own cash and stay within our means. If we can't pay cash for something, we don't buy it yet. We pay our vendors before the due date so that we can be debt free each day when we close our doors. The importance of creating a war chest or a rainy day fund is also vital for our people to see.

Seeing our financial statements is a great teaching opportunity for most of our people because they show how a company is run fiscally. Beyond the nuts and bolts of Fishbowl, however, I want all our employees to live by these principles, and for them to show their own progeny this example of living happily and within their means. I have witnessed families stay out of bankruptcy because of how they handled their finances. The more we teach our employees, the more they will be engaged in the welfare of our company and with one another, which fosters trust. Someday they may own their own companies—many of our employees already do, on the side—and the financial literacy that they gain while working at Fishbowl will improve their propensity to succeed in their own investments and financial endeavors.

People are ready to trust one another; all they need is the right touch. I'll give you an example from my adventures with auto repair. When I recently helped a neighbor fix and start his 1985 Pontiac Grand Prix, I thought of how coaxing a balky engine back to life was analogous to leading, guiding, and loving people so they can engage and become robust—which I define as being able to work in any environment under any condition.

My old truck at the ranch sometimes needs a bit more convincing. Depending upon weather conditions, it takes just the right amount of pumping the gas pedal, turning the ignition, and prayer to turn the engine over without killing the battery or flooding the carburetor. It requires a special touch, some intuition about your vehicle, and a bit of consideration for the environment where it's kept—but once it starts, it's a robust performer.

Like so many things in life, it just takes faith to get my truck, or my neighbor's car, moving. This example can be used in so many ways in how we lead, support, know, feel, watch, learn, and then offer a prayer of gratitude for our people. Sharing the big picture with our employees jump-starts their belief in trust, which helps them become robust enough to keep things running and operating at high efficiency through all conditions in the Bowl.

OVERVIEW OF THE 7 NON-NEGOTIABLES AND THE STRUCTURE OF THIS BOOK

1. Non-Negotiable Retrospectives: Examining Respect, Belief, Trust, Loyalty, Commitment, Courage, and Gratitude
   a. Reflecting on the Attributes of the Non-Negotiables to Develop Your Soft Traits
   b. Learning from the Failing Up Chronicles and Creating Your Hard Results
   c. Discovering Opportunities Earned
2. Supplemental Exercises: Experiencing the 7 Non-Negotiables

THE 7 NON-NEGOTIABLES AND THEIR ATTRIBUTES

The foundation of Fishbowl is our 7 Non-Negotiables and their Defining Attributes:

Respect
Seek to understand others before you seek to be understood.

Belief
If you believe in yourself, you can Fail Up and overcome anything.

Trust
Trust is the foundation of healthy relationships and it must be earned.

Loyalty
Promises must be more than words, even if they require sacrifice.

Commitment
Hold nothing back and work like this is your last job.

Courage
Never back down from a challenge; find the strength to soar.

Gratitude
Seek opportunities to express kindness in word and deed.

Coming together is a beginning; keeping together is progress; working together is success.

—Henry Ford

Every day we have an opportunity to walk off our arrogance and tame our egos by keeping the issue the issue and offering the 7 Non-Negotiables to those we come in contact with.

The first step is to offer unconditional respect.

7 Non-Negotiables Team-Building Exercises

The exercises provided in this book demonstrate how the 7 Non-Negotiables are woven together. They were developed by our leadership team for our people, and we encourage you to use them to discover what inspires you and brings meaning to the 7 Non-Negotiables. We live in an active, ever-evolving Bowl, and we look forward to what the changing seasons will offer us. Exercises and workouts help us keep the 7 Non-Negotiables alive and vibrant.

We believe that most of the challenges that keep us from being our best at work can be solved on 3 × 5 cards. It is tough to scientifically engineer or over-architect a 3 × 5 card. Our Fishbowl team leaders create their daily work assignments on 3 × 5 cards and play games to teach our employees how to effectively use the 7 Non-Negotiables at work. Every year, we update, refine, and improve the game. You are welcome to play along with us by subscribing at www.7NNs.com.

As you read the materials, keep four 3 × 5 cards close with the following weekly retrospective questions to explore your thoughts.

Weekly Retrospectives: Explore. Dream. Discover.

1. What can I learn this week?
2. How can I grow this week?
3. What can I do better—in my personal life, in business, and on behalf of my coworkers, partners, and business community?
4. How can I create positive outcomes that benefit all?

> Twenty years from now you will be more disappointed by the things you didn't do than by the ones you did do. So throw off the bowlines. Sail away from the safe harbor. Catch the trade winds in your sails. *Explore. Dream. Discover.*
>
> —*Mark Twain*

Creating Your Personal Legacy

> You're writing the story of your life one moment at a time.
> —*Doc Childre, Founder of the Institute of HeartMath*

In building a business, we sometimes forget to respect one another's personal ecosystems. We spend a lot of time working to understand each other. When we are having a bad day, it's easy to forget to put some time between the stimulus and the response and clear out our feelings before taking action.

We encourage you to get out into the fresh air, move, and create someplace away from your office and computer. Creating breathing space is one of the best things that companies can do to create extraordinary work environments. The majority of our challenges have been solved not in the boardroom but by simply taking a break, going for a walk, and seeking to understand one another.

Every day you see someone who represents something you aspire to in life. Here is the secret-sauce recipe for getting to where you need to be:

$$Time + Action = What\ Shows\ Up\ in\ Your\ Life$$

Last, consider that our stories are our lives. Who is your favorite author? Who is the writer that best resonates with you? Have you considered that you are the author of your life and that you can write yourself a good life?

Non-Negotiable Retrospectives: Examining the 7 Non-Negotiables

The common denominator at Fishbowl is our 7 Non-Negotiables. As we master each Non-Negotiable, we move forward personally, inter-personally, and as a team. It is like oars in the water. They might not be moving in perfect rhythm, but they are moving us in the right direction.

Making a difference in your own life and ultimately in the lives of others begins with defining your Non-Negotiables and Attributes. Our team created a series of exercises to help you define the Non-Negotiables personally, interpersonally, and as a team. Getting started on this process may take some effort. Now it's time to start learning about the 7 Non-Negotiables and applying them.

1

RESPECT

REFLECT on the Attributes of the Non-Negotiable to Develop Your Soft Traits

LEARN from the Failing Up Chronicles and Create Your Hard Results

DISCOVER Opportunities Earned

No one can make you feel inferior without your consent.
                                                    —Eleanor Roosevelt

Reflecting on the Attributes of the Non-Negotiable: Developing Respect through Empathic Listening

The dictionary defines the term *keystone* as the "central stone at the summit of an arch, locking the whole together. The central principle or part of a policy, system, etc., on which all else depends." For Fishbowlers, the keystone of the 7 Non-Negotiables is *respect*.

Respect is essential in any relationship. It's something each individual involved needs to earn over time. In turn, the keystone of respect itself is listening—and making a habit of never talking about someone behind their back. You don't have to judge others for doing so; you can simply make it a practice in your own life not to participate in discussions about individuals who are not present.

Part of the building blocks of respect at Fishbowl is the importance of not just listening to one another, but listening *empathically*, which means much more than just listening until somebody is done speaking. It requires that you listen with your eyes directed at the speaker. It's listening to what they are saying without judging, without our natural tendency to try and figure out a response before they're even done speaking.

When it comes to empathy, one of our most important statements at Fishbowl is, "I've got your back." This phrase carries all the Non-Negotiables with it. It means that everyone is looking out for each other and trusting that everyone else is doing the same for them. Are we perfect? Of course not; no one is. But we do have the skills to get back on track—to course-correct and move forward.

Developing Empathic Listening Skills

When people talk, listen completely. Most people never listen.

—*Ernest Hemingway*

Truly empathic listening occurs when a person is fully engaged and aware that whomever he or she is speaking to is listening. It lets a speaker know that you are honoring them, which he or she then reflects back. This kind of reciprocal engagement always strengthens relationships. Here are some steps for becoming a great empathic listener.

Make authentic eye contact and turn toward the individual who is speaking, so they know you're listening to them. This kind of physical attention lets the other person know that you're not doing something else—looking around, typing, texting, or anything else besides listening fully.

Another aspect of empathic listening is waiting until the person is finished speaking to begin sharing your thoughts—which can be difficult if the individual has a lot to say. It's not necessarily a bad idea to say something like, "Can we stop here and take a little break?" or "Let me try to understand what you're saying" to get the conversation back on track. That's part of empathic listening—and it is still respectful when done properly. Repeat back what you think you heard the person say to make sure you interpreted what they are trying to communicate correctly.

These actions often take a conversation to an even deeper level because they help people clarify information, send the right messages, and/or provide another perspective. An engaging, respectful conversation involves seeking to understand before being understood. That is a "Covey-ism"; Stephen R. Covey taught frequently about empathic listening. We may not be as efficient when we take time to understand others fully, but we will be more *effective*. And we'll always strengthen our relationships if we follow this pattern.

Yet another tool that helps us to foster respect as an empathic listener—and beyond conversation, too—is to put some time between a stimulus and our response to it. Sometimes it only takes a few seconds to defuse the emotions it might evoke; other times, it can take a day or even a week.

For example, let's say I'm driving down the road and I get cut off. My natural tendency is to get upset at that person for being so disrespectful while driving. If I were to react immediately, I would do something that I would regret later, like press on the gas and pass the car, or look over at the driver and give them a stare—both of which are immature and sophomoric. However, if I just breathe deeply for a moment and ignore this person, the stressful emotion passes.

Think about how many times we do something similar at work. We get angry at a coworker over something small and let it ruin our entire day, or someone says something that hurts or offends us. However, if you just put some time between your initial reaction and your decision to do something about it, you'll be professional, mature, optimistic, and respectful. That doesn't mean you avoid the issue altogether; just that you air out a little bit before you say or do anything. Take some time to think about what you want to say so that you can say it clearly.

Keep in mind that respect is the keystone.

Then make sure that what you say and do is uplifting, which you can accomplish by listening effectively and seeking understanding. You may have misunderstood someone else's emotions or reacted inappropriately because what you thought you heard is not really what they meant—as is so often the case. Seek to understand their underlying meaning; you'll often find you misinterpreted it.

Once you put some time between the stimulus and the response, the next step toward listening with empathy is to make an effort to *seek to understand* him or her. This has always been a positive experience for me, and it can actually form a stronger relationship when you approach a person in this way.

Failing to go to the source and get to the bottom of things usually does more harm than good. If you hold the negative emotions within yourself, you harbor bad opinions and ill will against that person, which will only drive a wedge into your organization, hurting you and everyone around you. Though it's doubtlessly difficult, you must have the courage to share your thoughts and feelings with the individual. It's entirely possible to do so professionally. Approach the misunderstanding as a subject matter or an issue rather than a challenge. When you do it that way, great things can enter a relationship.

Because these principles are timeless and universal, the same is true when someone speaks about a department, employee, or project. They're not complicated or difficult to grasp; most of us practice them outside of work every day. Seek to understand the individuals who bring up issues, and take the emotion out of the situation.

The most destructive thing you can do to your relationship with someone is to speak rudely about them behind their back. This shows total disrespect for that person. However, the reverse of this—singing someone's praises to another person—is one of the greatest compliments they can receive. If, for example, I say something to Beatrice about Dusty and then Beatrice shares what I said about Dusty with him, he is going to feel fantastic.

Therefore, while you want to avoid complaining audibly about coworkers, feel free to share positive observations about them as often as possible. The more specific you can be, the better; maybe something about their leadership style that you particularly like, an action they took that you admire, or something you're learning from them.

Another principle of respect that can build empathy is to *keep the issue the issue*. Don't make it a personal attack. Keeping the focus on the problem at hand will help you overcome the fear that it might grow into something bigger and scarier than it really is. Human beings have a tendency to make things emotional when things seem daunting—and emotions are powerful. You want to avoid this, whether you're in a group of any size, or one on one.

A further tactic for empathic listening when discussing an issue with someone: *Sit on the same side of the table*. This promotes a sense of unity. You can look at the issue together instead of succumbing to the tendency to separate yourself from it. Lean toward the other person rather than away, but respect his or her personal space. If you need something physical to draw attention away from emotion, write the problem on a 3 × 5 card and place it on the table so you can keep the issue the issue. Now it won't be seen as a personal attack; instead, you're both looking at the same issue on the table as you sit on the same side.

SHOWING RESPECT

Another valuable Covey-ism: You cannot talk your way out of the things that you behaved yourself into. You have to behave your way out. This is also part of our Fishbowl Prime Directive. For example,

I recently received an e-mail from a person who I had not heard from in 15 years. This individual had done a lot of things to hurt me and people close to me. She was under the impression that a two-paragraph e-mail would wash everything away. I responded this way: "Thank you for your message. It's wonderful to hear from you, but one single document cannot take away the long-term collateral damage your behavior has caused. You can't, in an e-mail, talk your way out of things that you behaved yourself into for so many years." I also added, "However, the door is open," and that's how I left it. The principle I want to teach here is that once you've breached trust through your behavior, the only way to repair it is to behave your way back into trustworthiness.

People often believe that the things they've said to make amends are enough; but if their behavior doesn't match their words, then their words are essentially worthless. If you're going to say something, make sure you can back it up with your actions. Even better—*start* with your actions and let them do the talking for you.

If you allow harmful behaviors to continue in your organization by simply ignoring them, they will fester and eventually cripple your company. When individuals with whom you work say or do negative things that need to be addressed, *address them*. Do it in a respectful, empathic, and nonjudgmental way, but do it as quickly as possible. Your job as a leader is to be strong. When you know that a wrong has been done—something that defies your organization's principles and value system and that harms your people—you must show those following you that you will do everything in your power to correct it.

We at Fishbowl consider such a wrong to be anything harmful to our people *or* our customers. In cases in which someone says something rude or dishonest, or fails to do something they committed to do, they can't just say, "I'm sorry." Sorry is a start; but to truly make a difference, you must change your behavior and possibly make restitution and reparation. At times, you may need to work twice as hard to heal an offense—something that you neglected to do or attempted to minimize. Whatever it may be, a leader must feel comfortable addressing an issue that is disruptive or harmful to his or her company.

FAILING UP CHRONICLES: HOW WE CREATE WEDGES IN LIFE, AND HOW WE CAN MEND THEM

Some of my fondest memories as a young boy are of the time I spent with my grandfather, Karl Williams (all five feet of him), on our ranch in Canada. Though small in stature, he had the biggest heart of any man I have ever known. The highlight of our summers together was when we chopped wood. Our goals were usually to clear paths or get rid of dead trees and branches that had fallen. And in some cases we would knock down trees that were overgrown to thin out part of the forest.

One day, when I was in my mid-teens, I was out with my grandfather chopping wood. I was using an old ax, and the head broke off from the handle; fortunately we had another ax with us. I noticed a young, tender tree near where we were working, so I placed the ax head on its lowest branch until I could get to it later. But I forgot about it and left it behind.

Twenty-five years later, I was taking my son, Cam, to chop wood. I had brought our ranch truck to make it easier to haul the wood back to the cabin. As we worked, I suddenly heard a mighty crack—and watched as a huge aspen branch fell from 20 feet up. It startled us with its swiftness and force. Luckily, it missed us and the truck.

As my adrenaline level started to ebb a little, I wondered what had caused that branch to fall. I went over to the tree to investigate and, lo and behold, still attached to this big branch was the old, rusted ax head I had carelessly placed there a lifetime ago. Over time, the tree branch had weakened as it struggled to grow around the ax head. But no matter how big it got, it always had this weakness at its core that kept it from gaining strength—and no manner of growth could fix this deficiency. Eventually, the ax head had to be forcefully expunged from the tree—taking a whole branch with it. That's a lot of damage from such a small source. By a remarkable coincidence, I was present when this limb died as a direct result of my youthful actions.

REFLECTING ON LESSONS LEARNED

The ax head is analogous to emotional wedges that we sometimes drive into our relationships. And like the branch, time can cause those relationships to die—because we're carrying something around that we don't need that is slowly damaging us and sapping our strength.

We put ax heads into a relationship when we fail to meet our commitments or are disloyal. Even a small misstep can erode the strongest relationship if left untreated. Some problems aren't solved by the passage of time alone; they require us to act swiftly to repair and prevent further damage by talking it through, apologizing, and doing whatever it takes to put things right.

The tree wasn't entirely dead in my example; however, it lost a major stabilizing part of its structure. I've watched it in the years after this incident, and I've noticed that it now tilts away from where the limb was. It looks rather precarious. The absence of its limb is throwing the tree off balance—which may well lead to more serious problems down the road. That's another lesson we can learn from this experience: Damaging one relationship can throw other parts of our lives into disarray as we try to compensate for the loss.

Write down the most important lessons you learned from the Respect Non-Negotiable and how you can apply it in your life.

1. _____

2. _____

3. _____

4. _____

5. _____

6. _____

7. _____

BUSINESS APPLICATIONS

We can proactively search for these ax heads in a business setting—places where we feel fear, stress, or doubt. Fear is an enemy to all the Non-Negotiables. When you care about a relationship, you don't let misunderstandings and bitterness get in the way. Instead of getting angry, take a moment to look for ax heads—both within your heart and in others'. That will allow you to confront the real issues instead of attacking people.

If you find that you inadvertently placed ax heads into colleagues, employees, customers, or even leaders, have enough courage to talk to them about it. Push your ego aside and apologize for the offense, whatever it may be, so that you can remove the ax head before it festers and causes a permanent wedge in your relationship.

The other interesting element of the story is that the ax head was still attached to the tree, even though the limb had died. I actually had to use a rock to get it off the tree, which clearly shows that the longer we wait to repair a relationship, the harder it becomes to do so. If you discover that you've offended or hurt someone, you should *welcome* the opportunity to have that individual share their feelings with you. Such encounters may even prompt these relationships to grow into some of the longest-lasting, deepest, most profound connections that you will have in life, all because both parties embraced the opportunity to remove their ax heads.

PERSONAL APPLICATIONS

When my son, Cam, passed away, people wanted to express words of sympathy and support. As a result, they often said things while still trying to work them out in their minds—usually something about their own loved ones who had passed. There are many reasons why people want to say something when their friend loses a loved one—particularly a child, which is a stunningly sad event for a family.

But because of their need to say *something* to me, certain people made some very hurtful comments—albeit unintentionally. "Look on the bright side. Perhaps in time, you will see that this is a good thing," or "He's in a better place now. You will get over it." I knew these people did not mean to cause pain; their statements were just poorly worded and thought out. And despite my grief, I was able to think logically about what my friends were trying to say, and I forgave their mistakes while fortifying myself against such barbed balms in the future. I realized that these people wanted to show they cared—they just didn't know how to express it. When you establish relationships with people based on mutual respect, you can more readily forgive them when they make mistakes because you know what's in their hearts and you can assume they have the best intentions. Respect is a powerful foundation that is not easily broken. Before you can effectively give respect to others, you must first respect yourself, as I'll discuss next.

SELF-RESPECT

If you don't read anything else in this book, I hope you will read this small section on self-respect. It helped transform our company in many ways. Life got better in the Bowl when we discovered that we could offer the 7 Non-Negotiables to others and stop expecting the world to pick up the slack for us. We could offer ourselves unconditional respect. We could believe and trust ourselves. We could stand strong for what we believed in and what we committed to. Because our environment was supportive, courage and gratitude grew organically. We stopped looking to the world to provide what can truly only come from the inside. This was the key that helped us stop seeing our world as limiting or judgmental. We stopped taking small issues personally. We learned that if we wanted to be happy in the Bowl, it had to start with respecting ourselves and others.

Real self-respect comes from dominion over self. If our motives, words, and actions are dictated by forces outside of us rather than from within, others will sense our insecurity or duplicity.

The view we have of ourselves affects not only our attitudes and behaviors but also our views of other people. In fact, until we take how we see ourselves—and how we see others—into account, we will be unable to understand how others see and feel about themselves and their world. We will most likely blindly project our intentions on their behavior and think ourselves objective.

I love how Goethe puts it: "Treat a man as he is, and he will remain as he is; treat a man as he can and should be, and he will become as he can and should be." This isn't to say that we trust him unconditionally, but it does mean that we treat him respectfully.

Some people say that you have to like yourself before you can like others. Okay, but if you don't know yourself, if you don't control yourself, and if you don't have mastery over yourself, it's hard to like yourself, except in some superficial way. We don't focus much energy on liking ourselves or trying to be perfect. Less really *is* more in the Bowl.

Jim Rohn said it best: "Don't wish it was easier; wish you were better." Every day presents this opportunity. Every day also presents opportunities to feel doubtful, unappreciated, and undervalued. It's your choice. Offer the 7 Non-Negotiables to yourself whenever you feel your energy and vitality decreasing. Go for a run, disrupt the thought pattern, and get back in the game. To this end, we encourage all of our employees to adopt a healthy and energized lifestyle. To get outdoors and play and laugh often. Our best ideas were never produced in a boardroom—in fact, we don't even have a boardroom at Fishbowl. We work in an open-air environment on a technology campus that formerly housed WordPerfect and Novell. We respect those who came before us and what they built. We also loved tearing down all the walls that separated the offices in the 1980s and 1990s. Open space and open minds create collaboration that leads to developing extraordinary outcomes.

HARD RESULTS FROM SELF-RESPECT

Leaders, have you ever really seen a member of your team lit up? Have you created an environment where you can see the passion in the belly? An employee shared with us that when he began taking care of himself, he took better care of others. He lost more than 50 pounds and committed himself to living a healthy lifestyle. He also transformed himself at work and today is one of our finest leaders.

In our early years, we adopted the standard developer lifestyle. We ate a ton of pizza and energized on Mountain Dew, and everyone had a desk full of candy bars. We entertained ourselves with a steady diet of video games. But we began to notice that the overall energy and vitality of our company was diminishing. So, as leaders, instead of taking things away, we chose to up our game. We started providing healthy food options. We took the time to shop for fresh food instead of offering catered meals. We enjoyed outdoor barbecues and in-house luncheons where the leaders did all the cooking. We also sponsored sporting events like mountain hikes, soccer and basketball teams, marathons, and Ultimate Frisbee.

The vitality of the Bowl not only returned; it began to flourish, and so did our people. We believe the only way for a company to adopt a health and wellness program is for the leaders to live and practice what they preach. For additional information on how Fishbowl implements and maintains health and wellness programs, go to www.7NNs.com.

WORK ENVIRONMENT APPLICATIONS

No one comes to work saying, "I want to hurt my coworkers or denigrate my company today." Most of the time, it's just a misunderstanding or an innocent mistake. If we as leaders forgive others and seek to understand the things that seem so hurtful in the moment, we can soar even higher—and, perhaps even more important, find immense satisfaction in our work. We can forgive one another, put our egos aside, move on, and continue working together as a team.

Why is it so important to learn to be respectful and look past emotions to find solutions? If you don't learn this lesson, it doesn't matter how many jobs you take; the same weakness will remain inside you like a ticking time bomb. Finding a new job won't fix your problems; it will just transfer them to a new location. If you find yourself wanting to leave a job over disagreements or hurt feelings, take a step back and consider what you can change about *yourself* to find a satisfactory resolution. However, if you can master your emotions and consistently strive to build strong relationships, you will reap the benefits of respectfulness and long-term happiness.

SUPPLEMENTAL MATERIALS AND EXERCISES TO DEVELOP YOUR OWN NON-NEGOTIABLES AND DEFINING ATTRIBUTES

The Attributes of Respect

1. Seek to understand others before you seek to be understood.

2. Treat one another with compassion, understanding, and kindness.

3. Respect others' ideas, time, and priorities.

4. Be thoughtful. Consider your actions. Think of others. Seek opinions about your ideas, and listen carefully to the responses. Gather data. Be methodical when taking action. Be careful in your job. Think of customers *and* coworkers.

5. Show high regard in both attitude and behavior toward coworkers, customers, products, and the space you work in.

6. Treat others kindly for who they are today, and keep in mind who they will become in the future.

7. Remain open to the fact that wisdom and innovation can come from anywhere. Silence your own opinion long enough to truly hear what others are saying.

COMPLETE THE FOLLOWING EXERCISES AND RETURN TO THIS SECTION TO ADD YOUR OWN NON-NEGOTIABLE AND DEFINING ATTRIBUTES

Enter your Non-Negotiable Value_____

1. _____
2. _____
3. _____
4. _____
5. _____
6. _____
7. _____

In seeking to understand, respect, and appreciate those who do not look, dress, behave, act, or think like we do, we authentically come to understand, appreciate, and learn from them, and ultimately learn to soar in all aspects of our lives. When all 7 Non-Negotiables are working within you in unison, you will begin to fire on all cylinders.

Everyone creates in a unique and remarkable way. You will also discover that when you create something positive, you have two choices: You can take all the beauty that has been created and swallow it down to feed your ego, or you can share it. This exercise is a game changer. You are learning how to rise above judgment that would have incapacitated you in the past, what you are ready to be free from within yourself and—perhaps most important—when you discover the gold within, how to not let your ego run wild with it. We are human, and most humans are born with a self-centered instinct. What we don't realize is how it incapacitates us. When we swallow all our achievements for our ego, no one ever sees the magnificent fireworks show. All they see is how ego shows up in the game of work.

The business world sends us mixed messages: "You must achieve to remain on the team. You must demonstrate every day how you add value." Yet when you achieve and demonstrate you are a rock star, you are labeled as someone who isn't in it for the team. This is a frustrating paradox, and it's a game in which everyone ultimately loses. It's time for a new game with simple rules that yield magnificent outcomes.

Our lives are enriched when we can erase judgment and remain open to letting the tender mercies and miracles flow in when they are ready. There can come a day in your life when you are free of all judgments if you keep working at it. We begin to develop deeper levels of awareness from our successes and Fail-Ups. Everything simply produces outcomes, and we become effective in all aspects of our lives when we can view the outcomes objectively.

This is also a good time to take stock (after all, we *are* inventory people) and think back on our world of work to see whether the same results keep showing up over and over again. We all go through seasons in our lives when it feels like we are just putting out fires. We eventually discover that it is almost always our actions that started those fires. We choose where we go to work and who we work with. The challenges/learning opportunities have always been there. The moment of clarity comes when you discover that the only person who needs to change is you.

Here are some of our Fishbowl exercises to help you get started. Our goal is simple: We want a positive and uplifting place in which to work and create. The far side of complexity is simplicity.

You don't need to keep your résumé up to date for your next big gig. You can show up tomorrow and build, develop, and grow right where you are. It's about you—not your environment. These steps can help you build respect for your peers and yourself:

Seven Steps to Establishing Respect

1. When you make an uncomfortable judgment, instead of burying it, see it as an opportunity to develop, learn, and grow.

2. Accept accountability for it, ask for understanding and forgiveness if necessary, and keep moving forward.

3. Write the judgment on a 3 × 5 card, along with three or more things that you can own about the judgment. Example: "I don't like Janice because she is unkind, talks behind my back, won't take the time to understand me. She won't help me achieve my goals on the team, and this causes me great stress and anxiety."

4. Turn the card over. Pause and take a breath, to put a few moments between the stimulus and the response. Mentally surround the individual (Janice, in this case) with the 7 Non-Negotiables.

5. Turn the card back over. Place a line through Janice's name and add yours. This provides you with an opportunity to stand in her shoes as the one being judged. "I don't like that I am unkind to Janice, and I don't take the time to understand her and help her to achieve her goals."

6. Ask yourself: Could my judgments about Janice be just as true about me? Get ready to discover something within yourself that you are ready to investigate and learn from. Write this down.

7. To disrupt your train of thought and open a new wavelength of thought, make a healthy deposit into yourself by doing something kind for another.

   Extra credit: If you are really brave, you can choose to do something nice for Janice. If you're not there yet, choose another work associate. Refocus your intent and energy to higher ground, or as we call it at Fishbowl, Courage Above Mountains.

TEAM RETROSPECTIVES

Twice a month, get together with a small group and share what you have learned about yourself and about respect through these exercises. This changes the paradigm at work to focus on development and learning instead of finger pointing, judgment, and blame—the no-possibility game. We all come up short from time to time. We all have human moments, lose our tempers, and feel doubt, fear, and defeat. At Fishbowl, we are thankful for the opportunity to do a little bit better every day.

2

BELIEF

REFLECT on the Attributes of the Non-Negotiable to Develop Your Soft Traits

LEARN from the Failing Up Chronicles and Create Your Hard Results

DISCOVER Opportunities Earned

The future belongs to those who believe in the beauty of their dreams.

—Eleanor Roosevelt

REFLECTING ON THE ATTRIBUTES OF THE NON-NEGOTIABLE: USING THE FIVE R'S TO FOSTER BELIEF

Building successful relationships with employees begins with believing in them, sometimes even before they believe in themselves.

Many individuals suffer from the common workplace fear that even if they work hard and stay at a company faithfully through good times and bad, they still might be expendable at the first sign of revenue loss. Some worry that they will never be as valued or well-compensated as newer employees. They therefore believe the only way to significantly increase their wages is to job-hop and hope for the best someplace else.

How can employers resolve these concerns? How can we, as leaders, demonstrate that we are as dedicated to our employees as we hope they'll be to us? We have developed the following five R's to give our employees a greater level of assurance about their commitment to stay:

1. *Responsibility:* Show your employees you trust them by giving them responsibilities that empower them and allow them to grow and feel like an important part of the company. Encourage them to gain new skills, competencies, and capacities by hiring from within wherever possible and by giving promotions at appropriate times.

2. *Respect:* Employees want to know you both respect them as people and appreciate the contributions they make. If you take their efforts for granted or fail to acknowledge them because you're too busy or distracted with your own concerns, they will likely start to feel dissatisfied—and begin to look elsewhere for the respect they desire. Treat every single employee, regardless of their position or tenure with the company, with respect.

I know of a CEO who regularly berates his employees in front of clients without warning. It is his way of trying to impress clients with his disdain for the slightest slip in performance. In conversations with other executives, he regularly refers to his employees as "the worker bees." Not surprisingly, turnover is rampant at his company.

Contrast this to another CEO's approach. While walking past an elevator with his board of directors, he noticed an employee in the elevator who had come to work despite the fact that he was clearly feeling bereaved over a family concern. He stopped the conversation, left his directors, and took the employee's hand in both of his while he expressed his sincere compassion for the individual. He made sure the employee was taken care of before moving on to his meeting. That company, not coincidentally, has extremely low turnover and is one of Utah's top revenue producers.

3. *Revenue Sharing:* Tie a part of your employees' wages to the company's performance to let them know that what they do *matters*. Offer a base pay and then add a part of the company's revenue and/or profit on top as a performance bonus. This will not only motivate the employees to work hard; it will also align their interests with the company's revenue and profit goals, and provide an incentive to stay with the company as it grows. The employees feel much more engaged and part of the company in this model, which is not all that different from company ownership itself.

This is an effective way for small businesses with high growth potential to attract top talent without breaking the bank. It also allows you to weather financial storms and reward employees generously during good times. By making the fixed cost of payroll more variable under differing business conditions, you can make your company more resilient and agile while treating your employees exceptionally well.

4. *Reward:* Though similar to Respect and Revenue Sharing, Reward goes beyond monetary compensation. While those elements are necessary to show gratitude for employees' hard work, other kinds of rewards contribute to the organization's positive atmosphere and serve as valuable morale builders. These include recognition in front of other colleagues, company and/or department parties, family events, Employee of the Month awards, free

lunches with the boss, gift cards, company logo clothing, thank-you cards, and flowers and support as employees grow their families, achieve personal successes, or do something good in the community.

5. *Relaxation Time:* Be generous with time off. Don't go overboard, but make sure your employees have sufficient time for sick days, family vacations, new babies, and other life events. Remember that it's their jobs that enable the company to grow; but also remember that they need to and *should* enjoy their lives when they're outside office walls. Your employees need to know that you honor and value the priorities they have in addition to their work-related responsibilities.

You need to require high-quality work from your employees; however, you cannot demand a continual level of pressure for them to perform at 100 percent. Give employees a chance to catch their breath as they move from one assignment to the next. You can help them do so by encouraging team-building activities and building break periods into the day. Keep objectives firmly in hand, but don't eliminate workday fun altogether.

The objective of long-term company commitment works both ways. It's understandable that employers look at least a bit askance at perpetual job hoppers. However, if you'd like your employees to make and keep a long-term commitment to your company, it is equally vital that you give them sufficient reason to stay.

Ask yourself the following two questions right now:

1. How do your leadership skills measure up in light of the Non-Negotiables discussed in this section—particularly in terms of a strategic perspective?

2. Would you rank yourself as strong, exceptionally strong, or as needing growth in the area of leadership?

Anyone who can pause and consider these questions is already well on their way to gaining a strategic perspective. And keeping this perspective in mind, the 7 Non-Negotiables are the natural follow-ups—they are necessary elements on the ensuing path to success.

FAILING UP CHRONICLES: LOSING A JOB AND GAINING A CAREER

Although I've mentioned him already in the book, I haven't yet shared that Stephen R. Covey was a mentor, a friend, and, at one time, my boss. This is why his teachings are woven into my DNA. Yet my path is and will always be distinctly my own. Stephen touched millions of lives, and allowed me to participate in this when I helped to open the First Things First Division of Covey Leadership in the 1990s. My time with the Covey Leadership organization helped to shape and mold me and is an integral part of who I am today. Stephen believed in his message, and his word was his bond.

We at Fishbowl believe in one another in much the same way. We are, perhaps, a little less perfect than some of Stephen's other students; but that is the one quality that most of us at Fishbowl embrace as our core. We don't quite fit the mold; yet rather than conform to any standard method, we've created our own unique style and brand. Many of us have been ceremoniously and unceremoniously asked to exit former places of employment. I understand the hurt and fear that many of our employees feel when they don't agree with something they see taking place at an organization. At Fishbowl, I have always respected those who have come in, closed my door, and shared their concerns.

My time at the Covey Leadership organization was remarkable. When the company announced it would merge with Franklin, I was open about my less-than-enthusiastic feelings concerning this move. I let my leaders know that I would be moving on, but assured them that I would work to ensure a smooth transition. Imagine my surprise and hurt when a few days later, I drove up to work to find all my belongings sitting in a box outside of a building I had loved and called home for many years. The pain of knowing that my former coworkers were watching from the windows while I collected my things and walked away is still hard for me to express.

How did I Fail Up from this experience? Time has healed the wounds and allowed me to appreciate how daunting it is to stand up for what you believe in. Our employees often tell me that I can be daunting, too. Yet they know that I will always listen to them—as long as they act from the keystone Non-Negotiable of Respect and make me aware of what they believe is best for the overall good of Fishbowl.

I was able to move on from this experience, and I continue to respect Stephen and the now-merged Franklin Covey organization. In fact, Stephen lived up the street from me for 22 years; he wasn't just a boss, but a neighbor and a friend, as well. A part of Covey Leadership's DNA will always be with me, and I've learned countless lessons since then, a few of which I would like to pass on here:

1. Don't judge a company or organization based on the actions of a few individuals within it.

2. There is *never* a good reason to be unkind. You can never justify an attempt to rob someone of their respect and dignity. If you must ask someone to leave your organization, do so with dignity and respect. Do not speak ill of the individual at any time.

3. Create organizations where individuals can safely voice their concerns. Not everyone is going to like or agree with you, but you can still offer kindness, understanding, and compassion.

4. Failing at a job doesn't mean life is over. Own it, learn from it, and move on. Perhaps one day you can even write a book about it.

REFLECTING ON LESSONS LEARNED

In some ways, this Failing Up experience prepared me for the next challenge I'd face—a personal earthquake that seemed to shake the ground beneath me. My life would get much worse before it got better. I understand now that all these events were preparing me to lead a little company called Fishbowl. I am not the only one in the Bowl to have lost a child. And I'm not the only one who has lost a job, blown a project, or experienced health challenges.

Thankfully, at Fishbowl we don't have to face these challenges alone. We believe in one another sometimes more than we believe in ourselves. We lift one another when we fall. There have been individuals who have left Fishbowl, and they have all been treated with kindness and respect. Many who have moved on from Fishbowl visit regularly and even operate Fishbowl Inventory software for some of our customers or for their own businesses.

After leaving Covey, I became a full-time entrepreneur. I made—and lost—a lot of money; but, most important, I *learned* a lot, as well.

The most memorable event of this venture for me occurred when I put everything on the line to relocate a large steel mill. My partners and I had put together a magnificent deal. All the pieces fit perfectly—in fact, so perfectly that the "debtor in possession and the lame duck" organization with whom we were working for two and a half years came to us one day and said, "We love this idea. We love it so much, in fact, we are going to do it ourselves. We really don't want an outside organization to help us."

I walked away from that meeting more than $1 million in debt and with no business assets to pay it off. This was one of the lowest points of my professional life. For a few weeks, I could barely get out of bed because of the heavy stress on my shoulders. I spent a lot of time on my knees and in quiet retrospection. I agonized over what to do. I knew I had a few options. I could file bankruptcy and leave those who invested with me hanging; or I could accept responsibility for the sudden turn of events, start over, and work to pay everyone back.

I met with some of my closest friends: two attorneys who I completely trust. I counseled with other associates, some who had gone through bankruptcy. I weighed all the pros and cons of declaring bankruptcy, and kept getting the same message from people: "You have perfect credit, you had good intent, and you did nothing wrong—and that's what the bankruptcy laws are for." It made sense on paper; but I would start to feel sick about it when I imagined actually going through with it. I felt as though it was wrong, somehow, and that there had to be another way. But I didn't know what that could possibly be.

I didn't have a job or any income during this time. I was trying to figure out a way to save the local farms that had been involved in the project. I felt an urgency to do something—quickly.

Then one evening, I had an experience that gave me the confidence to ask for more time from the creditors—and somehow had a feeling that they would give it to me. I'd never really thought about things from their perspective. I knew I needed time, and I didn't know how I was going to pay them back the money I owed them. I didn't even have a plan at that point. But I felt confident for some reason that asking for time would be the answer, even though I thought it would take the rest of my life. I was so convinced, in fact, that I woke up the next morning as early as I could to call the 180 people and entities to which I was indebted. By the end of my phone call with each, there was not a single person who didn't agree to give me time. Some weren't exactly pleased when I confessed that I didn't know how I was going to do it; but I agreed in writing what I would pay them back in some way every month. I promised to do my absolute best.

About half of my debts were to credit card companies; the other half were to individuals, banks, or other entities. I started whittling away at them bit by bit. I sent out e-mails and letters keeping everyone posted, and kept track of what I owed on a spreadsheet. It was incredibly exciting for me to watch my debt shrink each time I made a payment. It showed that I was making progress toward my ultimate goal of being debt free.

One day, I received a call from a close friend who had counseled me. He told me about a medical equipment company based in Salt Lake City that needed a good marketing/sales mind to help them expand nationally. I met with the company owner, and heard about how his organization retrofitted gamma cameras and resold them to hospitals and cardiologists. They were looking for someone who could sell to large hospital chains and who knew how to work with big contracts.

I remember the day I visited the company. I was in no way completely back on my feet. In fact, it was hard to even get out of bed in the morning. I sat with the group around a conference table, and someone said to me, "We hear you can do a lot of great things for our company and we'd like to have you do that." I confessed, "I don't know how much I can even work per day"—and then shared a little bit of my story with them.

To my surprise, the company owner simply replied that I should work however much I could, and he would start paying me per month. He was incredibly fair to me and presented me with an opportunity when I needed it most. I was thankful that someone still believed in me because I had stopped believing in myself.

I began working from home, and it was like starting over in college. I cold-called cardiologists and hospitals and tried to meet with their sales technologists to sell them gamma cameras. And little by little, I started to succeed and with that income I began whittling down the debt. I set up appointments and started making sales. These small achievements let the Salt Lake City-based company see that we could begin expanding and selling their product nationwide. Though they had mainly sold in Utah and Idaho in the past, I opened their eyes to the ability to do so on a much larger scale.

The company started to hire technicians around the nation to service the gamma cameras that they sold and installed. That gave me a few months to work things out with my creditors. What I earned from the medical equipment company gave me my confidence back—something for which I'll forever be grateful to the owners of that company. I proved myself with them for a couple of years and created relationships with the large original equipment manufacturers: Philips, Siemens, and General Electric. We worked with them and established mutually beneficial relationships between these manufacturers and the medical equipment company. Ninety percent of the income from this job went toward paying my debts; as my income picked up, I was able to pay more. I was also working as a consultant for several other companies, which provided a bit more income. It was hard, but little by little, I was getting back off the ground.

One of the most important lessons that I learned through this experience was to be less critical of other people who experience hardships. In the past, whenever I'd encountered someone with a business problem—someone who was too tired or beaten down to keep going—I'd think, "Are you kidding me? Get up and get back to work!" I had no idea how devastating this kind of blow could be to your energy and self-worth until I experienced it firsthand. I now realize that these people need a helping hand, a kind word, and other motivating factors to help them work bit by bit to lift themselves up.

I was grateful for the chance to work and pay back my creditors. Some were not as tolerant as others. Six months after I asked for their patience, a few demanded immediate payment in full. So I had to renegotiate terms that would accommodate them and still be possible for me to handle. It took me three years to pay off all of the money. I didn't miss a single payment; I even overpaid when I could. Some people were shocked that I had paid them back rather than going bankrupt.

There was one bank with which I had three leases and owed about $150,000. By the time I had whittled that down to about $30,000, the gentleman with whom I corresponded there had become a friend. He would often call me out of the blue, and at first I assumed, "Well, of course he's calling to check up. He probably just wants more money." But I realized after a while that he was just calling to see how I was doing and say hello because he was delighted and amazed that I was still keeping up with my obligations years later.

One day he called and said, "I've been talking with my managers about your situation. We decided that since you've made such great progress when we didn't think we would receive anything back, we'd like to write the last thirty thousand dollars off. We have agreements drawn up and all you need to do is sign those so we can close the account. Is that okay with you?" I remember putting the phone on my leg and weeping. I got back on the phone and simply said, "Of course. Thank you." That was just one of the many miracles that came as a result of this situation.

But the greatest miracle was that *everyone was paid every penny.*

Of course, I had to pay some interest, but I had negotiated a flat rate with those who required it (like credit cards) so it wouldn't keep accumulating. They all agreed to keep it low to allow me to get ahead and continue to pay regularly. Every single credit card company agreed to hold still on the interest as long as I paid my monthly payments and never missed one—and I didn't.

It might sound a little crazy, but by the time I paid the last credit card off, I was thankful to have had this experience. I wanted to have a credit-card-burning ceremony to announce to everyone, "This will never happen again. I will never have a credit card balance again."

But I decided to keep the cards. They serve as a reminder of what not to do in the future, and of what I was able to do with a lot of people's help and—without question, in my mind—divine intervention.

I also felt blessed to be able to share this experience as a lesson for fellow Fishbowlers. Fishbowl President Mary Michelle Scott describes this experience:

> Leaders teach employees through their actions more than through their words. David shared this personal experience with every member of the organization so they would understand in their bones what it means to be debt free. Even though the experience had completely broken David, he emerged from it stronger than ever. I can remember the first company meeting. David didn't show up as the traditional all-powerful CEO with projections and plans and presentations. He showed up in front of the group carrying a small brown paper bag; none of us knew what was in it. It turned out to be the credit cards that he had paid off one hundred percent over three years. To watch that personal story transform our Fishbowlers was a defining moment; it allowed our employees to fully understand for themselves what David had learned the hard way. It emphasized why it was so important that his word is his bond—and that Fishbowl remain debt free. All of the employees understood at that point why we chose to pay off our million-dollar bank loan as quickly as possible. We came together as a stronger and more unified team on that day.

My motivation for this presentation was to teach people at Fishbowl two things:

1. There's value in avoiding debt.
2. There's serious risk to your relationships and other aspects of your personal life when you're under its burden.

You're liberated when you have no debt. I wanted to send that message and share the elation I felt after paying every creditor off. I had accomplished something that would have seemed impossible to anyone else, even to people who knew that I worked hard and could do things well. They all advised me to file for bankruptcy; not one person told me to hang in there and pay it all off. The sense of accomplishment, and the fact that I can look at anyone in this world without ducking or hiding because I did not pay them what I owed them, is so important to me. Yes, it took a long time; but they got their money back. I even paid extra to some individuals, since I had the means and the desire to provide a little bit of interest on the time that it took. Two people actually came back and returned the extra money because they would not take interest from me.

We wanted to teach our employees at Fishbowl the principle of living debt free. This experience motivated me to operate our company without debt, which was crucial for our employees to understand and support. There have been many temptations to get lines of credit to grow the company faster; but the process I endured over three years of paying people back made it easy for me to say, "No, we'll grow with our own cash at the pace that we can." Fortunately, it's been a good, brisk pace most of the time. We had a couple of slower years, but we were still investing in our infrastructure and people, even though we weren't making much money.

That's the great lesson I learned from the steel mill adventure that I carried forward into Fishbowl. Going back to what I say to investors: "We are employee owned, debt free, we grow with our own cash, and our exit strategy is death."

The experience with the steel mill and medical company also ultimately led me to Fishbowl. While I was working at the medical equipment company, I would occasionally hear people utter the word "Fishbowl" with a negative connotation. At the time, I didn't know what they were talking about, but it usually came more from the employees, about the fact that the company owners were investing so much money into Fishbowl. The employees thought that money should be going to help their own organization rather than being invested in another entity.

On October 1, 2004, I was asked to take a look at Fishbowl. After the owner had invested millions of dollars in the company—10 times as much as he had planned—he wanted to stop the bleeding. He had been promised that a product would be delivered to him at an earlier date, and he had been patient for a long time. He didn't say, "Go to Fishbowl and make my money back"; he said, "Go to Fishbowl and look through the operation, see what you can make of it."

There were six individuals at Fishbowl—a programmer, a tester, a former support tech, an operations guy, and two salesmen—all of whom were basically working for free since no money was coming in.

In the beginning, there was really nothing finished to sell. The product wasn't quite ready to go to market; however, the employees told me that they were almost there, and I believed them. I saw the sincerity in their eyes, so I asked the medical equipment company owner—who had sent me there in the first place, and who was Fishbowl's majority shareholder—to give me 30 days before shutting the company down. I promised that he would not have to put any more money into it. I wanted to see what we could do with it in 30 days. And somehow, we found a way to get a product ready for market within that short timeframe. Fortuitously, software company Intuit opened up its Marketplace around that time—a tool that was used for add-ons to their product, QuickBooks. It didn't take long for us to integrate our product with QuickBooks. We were soon up on their website—and when QuickBooks finally made their Gold, Silver, and Bronze Developer classifications, we were one of the first three Gold Developers Intuit crowned in late 2004. That put us in a great position on the website, and we got a lot of leads from it. Fishbowl took off—and we never looked back.

After we integrated with QuickBooks and became a Gold Developer, in the last two months of 2004 we sold $312,000 of product—enough cash to pay the employees and the rent. I went right over to the landlord, who I knew well enough to discuss the circumstances. He was a patient, gentle, and kind man who had allowed Fishbowl to stay even when we couldn't afford office space. After we began making money, we paid him everything that we owed within a month.

We then signed a new lease—a win-win situation for all involved. Since then we've been growing our lease and expanding our offices. In less than two years, we will purchase the entire building that Fishbowl calls home. There was still some debt to pay after earning that first $312,000. There were quite a few accounts payable that were past due; but we were debt free by the end of 2005's first quarter. We then began growing at a rate of 300 percent for the next few years.

Write down the most important lessons you learned from the Belief Non-Negotiable and how you can apply it in your life.

1. _____
2. _____
3. _____
4. _____
5. _____
6. _____
7. _____

BUSINESS APPLICATIONS: HOW TO BE THE WORST MANAGER—BUT THE BEST BOSS

The worst managers can make the best leaders. And a great leader can become the very best kind of boss. How can this be true? I'll explain.

To begin with, consider what a manager's role truly is. Their job is essentially to *accomplish work through others*. Managers instruct, supervise, motivate, evaluate, and mete out rewards and punishments. Some manage from behind by cracking the whip, micromanaging, and shouting orders in the same way cattlemen or shepherds manage: by fear, intimidation, and authority.

The first problem in this scenario is the way people come to be managers in the first place. Typically, managers are employees who are promoted because of their expertise in a certain subject matter.

They move up in an organization by becoming highly proficient in their original jobs.

Unfortunately, despite their skill in their previously held roles, they are generally untrained as managers. Many lack mentors or positive role models to guide them in this much different path. And even when companies provide training, it is generally schooling on the various facets of measuring work production and controlling employee behaviors (I refer to this as "managing from behind"). Little or nothing is taught about the character traits and values a company stands for, the ones it would seemingly want its managers—the face of the company for every employee within it—to represent and exude.

So what do these individuals do? They become terrible managers because they do the following:

- Micromanage
- Take credit for others' ideas and projects
- Create rules for the many that are meant to police and control the behavior of a few
- Make decisions that support their near-term compensation at the expense of the organization's long-term goals
- Hire and fire the wrong people for the wrong reasons
- Rule by force, fear, intimidation, and title

None of these approaches achieves anything positive. A team will naturally follow a leader who is willing to lead from the front, instead of drive from behind.

We could write many books on bad managerial behavior. In general, however, the result is the work environment we all know too well: fear, mistrust, worries over job security, and feelings of unfairness and ill will—and a terrible company culture.

WHAT CAN—AND SHOULD—BUSINESSES DO?

For one thing, they can take a cue from our company, where we have extended the principles of *Agile Development* into *Agile Leadership*. *Management* is simply not a word in the Fishbowl vernacular. We create paired leadership teams that guide and empower employees to do their jobs in the way they see fit. Our Captains work side by side with their teams, rather than directing and controlling them in a traditional sense. They lead from the front and set the pace. They show by example and their people follow.

Captains are terrible managers, but they are incredible leaders whose teams produce great results. Here are a few of the traits that can turn a seemingly terrible manager into an incredible boss:

1. *Trust your employees* to get their jobs done. No micromanaging allowed.

2. *Help others get ahead* when deserved, even at your own expense. What a novel idea! Don't concern yourself with climbing the corporate ladder. If your people and teams are successful, you'll naturally rise, as well.

3. *Give credit where it is due.* Don't take undeserved credit for others' work, however enticing the idea might be. It will not pay off.

4. *Set the strategy, but allow others to choose their own tactics.* It's amazing how empowering and motivating it can be when individuals get to manage the details of *how* they achieve a particular strategic goal. They will become unstoppable.

5. *Hold fewer (and more focused) meetings.* The fewer attendees you have at each meeting, the better. Define exactly what you need to achieve in each meeting, and stick to an agenda when you arrive.

6. *Celebrate failure and reward innovation.* Encourage team members to try new things, even when you know that they won't always produce perfect results. They *will* make mistakes— which are opportunities to learn and Fail Up. This will result in employees who are brave and excited to work.

7. *Be in the people business.* If your people know that you have their backs, trust them, and care for their well-being and their families, they will naturally be motivated to work hard for you.

How do you find individuals with this terrible-manager potential? Against prevailing wisdom, they may not be proficient (or even familiar) with the team's tasks. But they will be highly capable and teachable in the values your organization stands for. The rest will follow.

An anthropology graduate could become a development lead. A licensed attorney could lead a world-class sales organization. A culinary student could become a standout leader in customer support. An electrician could become a top sales executive. A banker could become a top account manager. The possibilities are endless.

Even if you are a terrible traditional manager, what could this bigger vision of leadership be accomplishing for your company . . . or for *you*?

EMBRACE DIVERSITY

On the surface, Fishbowl may look like your basic high-tech, knowledge-worker, white collar company. Nothing could be further from the truth. Everyone in the Bowl is unique and extraordinary in their own right. There is no one mold at Fishbowl. Our common thread is the 7 Non-Negotiables.

Leaders need to be open to the possibility of what can come from every person in the company, from the newest to the oldest, and from everyone who comes into your life. We should always be open to meeting new people. Maybe we'll become friends, business partners, or neighbors. Anyone can add value to you personally and through the vital roles they play. None of us knows everything; we can learn from everyone we meet. If we shut down the flow of new people into our lives, we may miss opportunities to affect and uplift others. Likewise, we should never think of ourselves as better than someone else. Only true equals can create.

SUPPLEMENTAL MATERIALS AND EXERCISES TO DEVELOP YOUR OWN NON-NEGOTIABLES AND DEFINING ATTRIBUTES

The Attributes of Belief

1. Take care to be a positive force. Make sure your intentions are known by others, and your actions will have a positive impact on others.

2. With heart and mind, hold out for the greatest possible outcome and be patient when things get difficult.

3. Believe in and live the company mission: why and how we do what we do.

4. All ideas have value. Be open to the concept that success can be achieved from many different perspectives.

5. Believe in the big picture.

6. Fishbowl is not just a company but a way of life, important to people and their success.

7. Believe change can and will happen. Michael Jordan said it best: "They told me I couldn't. That's why I did."

COMPLETE THE FOLLOWING EXERCISES AND RETURN TO THIS SECTION TO ADD YOUR OWN NON-NEGOTIABLE AND DEFINING ATTRIBUTES

Enter your Non-Negotiable Value_____

1. _____
2. _____
3. _____
4. _____
5. _____
6. _____
7. _____

How Belief Is Created and Sustained within Organizations

You need to believe you can achieve your goals—that change can happen. If you want to change something about yourself, start by believing it is possible. But more than just hoping that it will happen, it has to lead to action.

Individual Exercise

Select a trait or habit of someone around you whom you admire. This can be a new idea or one generated by another activity from this book. Write it on a 3 × 5 card in the following format: *"Belief* by *trait/habit."* For example:

- "Work can be fun [the belief] by saying 'Hi' to everyone and giving them eye contact and a smile [the habit]."
- "Be more outgoing [the belief] by using small talk with a new person each day [the habit]."

Tape it where you'll see it first thing in the morning (e.g., computer monitor at work or a mirror at home).

When you first see it, read the card OUT LOUD.

- This will be the test. If you can read the card out loud, then you have the start of a firm belief in what is written.
- Note: It doesn't say "whisper"; you need to read it out loud.

INTERPERSONAL/TEAM EXERCISE

Select a trait or habit of someone around you that your team admires. This can be a new idea or one generated by another activity from this book. Write it on a 3 × 5 card in the following format: "*Belief* by *trait/habit*." For example:

- *We can be more likable* by *not speaking ill of other people.*
- *Be more balanced* by *setting time aside each day for family, work, and personal needs.*

Tape it where everyone on the team can see it.

Once every day, get everyone together to read the card out loud, and have them share an experience they had about the trait or habit written on the card.

Even if a person didn't have such an experience for the day, he or she will need to say something. The mere act of talking leads to action. It can inspire them to pay more attention to the next day.

EXTRA CREDIT FOR CHAMPION PLAYERS

Post the 3 × 5 card where visitors can see it, too. Share it with at least one visitor a day.

When reading your card out loud, say it loud enough for the office next door to hear you.

3

TRUST

REFLECT on the Attributes of the Non-Negotiable to Develop Your Soft Traits

LEARN from the Failing Up Chronicles and Create Your Hard Results

DISCOVER Opportunities Earned

Do one thing every day that scares you.

—Eleanor Roosevelt

REFLECTING ON THE ATTRIBUTES OF THE NON-NEGOTIABLE: THE QUALITY OF OUR RELATIONSHIPS AND PROMISES

We must develop the capacity to see men not as they are at present but as they may become.

— *Thomas S. Monson, president of The Church of Jesus Christ of Latter-day Saints*

We at Fishbowl know how to measure the value of things for businesses across the globe. We also know that some things in life are unmeasurable and without equal—and we have discovered that these are the very things that can bring the heart and soul of a company to life. Why?

Because we are all in the people business.

We have weathered more challenges and storms than most companies. What sets us apart at Fishbowl has always been our willingness to be transparent in our journey. We own our failures, learn from them, and share them so that others can learn as well. We bounce back higher every time we fall. We also do not believe in treading water. Employees who remain in one place grow weary. We keep moving, creating, playing, and working. Every day presents a new opportunity. Our employees look forward to the tough calls, the challenging customers, and the constant push to keep our software relevant in the market.

QUALITY OF RELATIONSHIPS

To determine how you're doing with your Soft Traits, you must first assess the *quality of relationships* across your organization—leaders to employees, employees to leaders, employees to employees, and employees to customers. Do people in all these groups honor and respect one another? Or are they neglected and considered unimportant?

You'll always be able to see, hear, and feel when trusting relationships exist in organizations. A healthy organization is full of people who:

- *Are loyal* to one another. They keep their word and honor their journey.

- *Never judge.* You do not know what others are going through and what challenges they might be facing.
- *Laugh with (not at) others.*
- *Take issues directly to the source.* Don't talk behind others' backs.
- *Express genuine appreciation* up, down, and across their organizational structure.
- *Help others with critical tasks.* You don't hear, "That's not my job" in a successful organization. You hear, "We're in this together."
- *Recognize that people aren't problems*—problems are problems. People who have been hurt sometimes hurt other people. They need to see beyond the hurt and help others instead.
- *Smile frequently.* People should leave work better and happier than when they arrived.
- *Don't start sentences or thoughts with, "What's in it for me?"* but with, "How can I best serve you?"

QUALITY OF PROMISES

Strong relationships are based on trust—and organizations can build a culture of trust by cultivating honesty and integrity in workers' interactions. Here are questions to ask that will help you measure the quality of a company's promises:

- How committed are team members to keeping their obligations? If leaders and employees make and keep their promises, they'll see strong trust and respect across the organization. If they frequently make commitments but fail to keep them, they'll see frustration and self-serving behavior.
- Do employees hold peers accountable for their commitments? You want people to be direct and assertive when promises are missed, and quick to thank others when they're kept.
- What happens when circumstances cause people to fail to keep commitments? Ideally, the promiser should update all stakeholders who are affected so that they know well in advance.

- Do team members consider promises to customers to be no more and no less important than promises to peers?
- Is everyone at your organization willing to forgive themselves and one another?

FAILING UP CHRONICLES: SURVIVING A RECESSION AND LEARNING TO SOAR

The year 2010 found Fishbowl—and countless other companies—in the heart of the recession. No one knew how long it would last; companies were closing right and left. Even some of our customers couldn't manage to escape unharmed. At around this time, our majority shareholder asked me to sell the company or to pay him for his portion of it.

I knew that it was a tremendous opportunity. Fishbowl's original majority shareholder is an extraordinary man who had helped me at the lowest point in my life. He reached out to me when I was still reeling from my steel mill adventure, and gave me the chance to regain and rebuild my confidence.

However, timing for *this* particular opportunity was terrible because not only were we in the middle of a recession, but also because I was facing a series of physical ailments that had all seemed to come at the same time. I've always had an iron will, but if I didn't have an iron body to go with it, it wouldn't have mattered much—the physical side had to be there, too.

There's an important lesson to learn here: Success is in the preparation. By the time we need to act, the time to prepare is over.

We knew we had to have a great year in 2011 if we were going to survive as a company. We had been fairly stagnant in 2009 and 2010, but we were gearing up for a phenomenal 2011. We felt like we had the people and resources to pull it off. But my serious—and frequently life-threatening—medical issues had sent my life into a tailspin.

I was thrust into one such issue during our 2011 company kickoff meeting. Fortunately, I knew I could count on my team members and employees. Despite my absence, the rest of the company was committed to holding the meeting. Mary Michelle Scott was leading the charge as the brand-new president of the company, and the Captains rallied the troops and led the charge into the season.

My own personal healing experience left me wondering exactly how someone can best learn to trust others, especially if he fundamentally tends to mistrust them. If this is your typical outlook, you must find ways to allow trust to grow again. You can instigate this by allowing yourself to give people or organizations a chance to become trustworthy.

If you can forget the past, you'll be able to remain open to the possibility that you can change your underlying beliefs. Sometimes the pain we've endured when someone has breached our trust makes it hard to extend that trust again. And although it's easier said than done, we can *always* find a way to give people another chance. Perhaps it's as simple as offering feedback, forgiving, and moving on. Today is a new day, and you never know what can happen if you just give it a chance.

This is a great time for you to take note of how you have learned to Fail Up and soar.

Write down the most important lessons you learned from the Trust Non-Negotiable and how you can apply it in your life.

1. _____
2. _____
3. _____
4. _____
5. _____
6. _____
7. _____

Supplemental Materials and Exercises to Develop Your Own Non-Negotiables and Defining Attributes

The Attributes of Trust

1. Trust is the foundation of healthy relationships and it must be earned.

2. Innovation creates an environment where people accept themselves and others as a natural—and even necessary—part of the growth process. This attitude supports an environment where people work without fear and look forward to discovery.

3. Start by trusting yourself, then extend trust freely to others to create reliance within the team, department, and company, and with customers and anyone else involved.

4. Be quick to forgive others, to enable them to rebuild trust.

5. Provide people with the opportunity to solve problems, for their own personal growth as well as the success of the company.

6. Trust that the actions and decisions of those around us are the results of in-depth thought and a consideration of possible consequences.

7. Have confidence that others are doing the best they can with the knowledge, power, and resources they have been given.

COMPLETE THE FOLLOWING EXERCISES AND RETURN TO THIS SECTION TO ADD YOUR OWN NON-NEGOTIABLE AND DEFINING ATTRIBUTES

Enter your Non-Negotiable Value_____

1. _____
2. _____
3. _____
4. _____
5. _____
6. _____
7. _____

This activity is used to help you understand how trust is a key factor in finding success in different aspects of business, life, and relationships. Once you identify the relationships that are ubiquitous in your daily activities, analyze whom you trust and whom you do not. Then work on building trusting relationships in order to find success in life.

1. Create a list of critical decisions that are affecting your department, project, or stewardship.

2. Write every decision on a 3 × 5 card, and organize them into a single line from top priority down.

3. Choose the top five cards. On the back of each, write the names of five employees who will be most affected by the decision.

4. Consider your relationship with each of these people. Circle the names of the people you would absolutely trust to make the decision.

Fundamentally, trust is created in a relationship that is built on equal reciprocity. Achieving a reciprocally giving relationship implies that it is held together by strong emotional bonds of respect and friendship. Building these bonds is often a simple and organic process.

There is no better way to build trust between individuals than for them to spend time together. Some simple activities that engender trusting relationships include eating together often, sharing the same social activities, and working in close proximity. The intrinsic value of sitting around a table and eating dinner together as a family cannot be understated. It creates a positive venue for sharing, communicating, and supporting one another. This principle extends to the workplace. The same intrinsic value of sharing a meal together often creates a positive venue to defuse conflict.

Other social activities can build trust among family, friends, and coworkers. For example, playing games with your children provides positive reinforcement and boosts their energy. This practice applies to most aspects of life: The more positive energy you can generate, the easier it will be to deal with stress, solve problems, and create happiness. Ernest Hemingway said, "The best way to find out if you can trust somebody is to trust them." We agree with his simple yet profound statement.

4

LOYALTY

REFLECT on the Attributes of the Non-Negotiable to Develop Your Soft Traits

LEARN from the Failing Up Chronicles and Create Your Hard Results

DISCOVER Opportunities Earned

Let us rather run the risk of wearing out than rusting out.
                                          —Theodore Roosevelt

REFLECTING ON THE ATTRIBUTES OF THE NON-NEGOTIABLE: TWO FISH ARE BETTER THAN ONE

I share this chapter with my paired leadership partner, Fishbowl President Mary Michelle Scott. As I mentioned in Chapter 2, everyone in leadership roles at Fishbowl works with a paired partner. People often ask us, "How do you make this work?" In most organizations there is only one leader. Is it easier to have one top dog at the top? Yes—for the leader. But it's not about the leader; it's about the welfare of our company and the well-being of our people. It's better for an organization to maintain a balance at all levels within the organization. This chapter focuses on our hopes of inspiring and helping other leaders to better understand their roles within their organizations. Loyalty is the key Non-Negotiable that makes it all work.

A CEO or leader no longer needs to go it alone; in fact, I would recommend they don't. Mary and I have each other's backs in business—as do our other paired-partner Captains—and we both bring different ideas to the table to create a third alternative that is not my idea or Mary's but simply what is best for the overall long-term health of the company.

FAILING UP CHRONICLES: THE COURAGE TO LIVE DEBT FREE

Our darkest hour turned out to be a turning point for our company as we found ourselves in a precarious financial position. Through an abundance of miracles, we managed to save our company literally at the last minute.

SEPTEMBER 2010

As I mentioned in Chapter 3, our majority shareholder notified us in 2010 that it was time to pay him back his original investment in full. He had supported Fishbowl for many years and it was time to return his money. We committed to completing the process in 90 days.

Fortunately, Mary was acquainted with Fishbowl by the time that call came. About a week after I first met with Mary about spending a little bit of time at Fishbowl, I told her about the majority shareholder's request. Part of me was really nervous about finding the money that he required, keeping him happy, and keeping the company going during the darkest time of our country's economic crisis.

We moved forward with the full belief that we'd find a way to save our company in its original form. Mary came in with a fresh mind, and she gave me confidence that there was a good chance that we'd pull it off. It helped me to see the value of Fishbowl from someone who was bringing a fresh perspective. We never doubted that, even as a number of investors gave us proposals we couldn't accept. We didn't want to be owned by anyone outside the company, but the due diligence process of compiling all the information and reaching out to our contacts helped us determine the value of the company.

We started to whittle away at our list of 58 potential investors. We met with many people; groups came in or conference-called us every day. The one that came through was Zions Bank, one of the four banks that we had contacted. Interestingly enough, as the Zions Bank representative left, Mary pegged them as the one that would invest. I thought, "Well, that's interesting. I really liked them too, but many people showed interest"—although many of them withered when it came to putting a letter of intent together.

As Mary says:

> David's belief in Fishbowl was absolute. There was never a doubt in his mind that we would find the money and secure the company for the employees. He never focused his energy on the hopelessness of the recession. What you focus on grows. In 2010, many people focused on fear and loss and that is what they created. David had one official valuation document to support the worth of Fishbowl and an enduring belief in every individual who worked here. He saw the buyback as the one-time opportunity for the company to achieve employee ownership. When he spoke about Fishbowl to potential investors, it wasn't the valuation document that captured people's attention; it was the person presenting it. So many people were counting on him—the employees, his family, the bank, and

the majority shareholder—to put all the pieces together and his faith never wavered.

The 7 Non-Negotiables existed long before they were named. The first time I heard David say boldly to a venture capitalist who had agreed to fund Fishbowl, "No way are we creating a board that you can sit on and no way will we report to you. You can write the check and I will pay it back in full with interest and that's it," I smiled and thought, finally I am working with a courageous leader who values the people of the company more than the profit that exit strategies can bring. I was also impressed with how much he respected the original investor of Fishbowl. Ultimately, David was able to do right by the original investor, whom he loves and respects and by the people of Fishbowl. His loyalty never wavered, his faith never faltered, and he had a great team that backed him up every step of the way. We had no "plan B." We always planned and worked to win. As we worked through the list of potential investors we could meet with, we were also defining what the future of the company would be. Our top priority was that Fishbowl never lose its culture. Also, if Fishbowl could make it, so could our partners and customers. We never missed an opportunity to remind Fishbowl's customers that they would come out of the recession seasoned and wise. I had a good feeling that Zions would take care of the good people of Fishbowl. Zions is an investment organization that has helped countless organizations transform into remarkable companies that enrich the community. I was also impressed with the dedication and commitment of the leaders who rallied around David and the company.

Meanwhile, the clock was ticking away. After several months of meeting with investor after investor, we opted not to further pursue venture capital funding. We realized that we would never dig ourselves out that way. All we needed was a loan. I had contacted people of great net worth who had the cash for a loan, but at that time, those who had cash really were kings. They were out buying properties and doing all sorts of things to make incredible returns, but we wanted a long-term loan with a very small interest rate. As the weeks went by, I kept in contact with the majority shareholder to let him know about the verbal offers and valuations that people were giving us—but we had nothing in writing yet.

December 2010

Zions Bank got back to us in the first half of December after completing their due diligence. They said that they could give us a loan for part of the majority shareholder's buyout price, which would let us retain the company for the employees.

This offer was verbal, so we kept waiting. Then it was the end of December and Fishbowl was trying to break even for the year. Prior to Mary's joining Fishbowl, I made the decision to optimize our online advertising campaigns so we got the best ROI for our PPC and SEO efforts. I took one of my biggest leaps of faith since I've been here by increasing the spending rate in this area. That decision has since paid off enormously, but at the time it was pretty daring and took a lot of courage. I felt right about it and trusted our team to manage those resources with great care.

As this was taking place, our list of potential investors that we started with had been cut down to nearly zero. We had contacted or met with everyone, and all we could do was wait. The last one standing was Zions, and they had told us verbally that a deal was coming, which we really trusted. We had high confidence that Brad Adamson, the senior loan officer we met with, would put a deal together. He said that they liked what they saw, but he hadn't committed to any particular amount.

We didn't have to reduce wages or lay anyone off during this time, so that was a miracle in and of itself. But my greatest motivation was for our people; I wanted to protect them. Our greatest fear had been that Fishbowl might be sold off in pieces, or be purchased by someone who didn't know how to run it and saw it only as an investment.

December 30, 2010, 5:58 pm: D-Day

On December 30, at 5:58 pm—the last day by which the majority shareholder had allowed me to come up with at least a letter of intent, and two minutes before the deal would be over and he could've pulled the plug—we got it. We received the letter of intent in the nick of time, and it provided us enough funds to buy out the shareholder. He believed in us and was even willing to carry some back in a second position.

APRIL 2011

If something could go wrong this month, it did. We posted our lowest sales numbers and heard the word "no" more than any time in the history of our company. Nothing seemed to be going our way. Our support teams were inundated with customer calls as the economy began picking up and businesses started using the software again. And my health deteriorated as a brutal combination of physical problems suddenly hit me. My back and left leg were completely numb and I needed back surgery, but first my appendix ruptured, and the nerve in my arm backfired, and a host of other ailments showed up. On top of this, there had been no word from the banks and we had no other options. If there were ever a month to call it in and give up, April would have been perfect.

The one thing we didn't do was give up. Even during our most challenging times, all of our employees stayed with the company. My advice to leaders, therefore, is when the going gets tough, just hang in there. You don't have to get tougher. Just remain focused and stay the course. There is no need to upset the ship by causing unnecessary waves in your respective Bowls. This is where our term "Don't tap on the glass" comes from.

MAY 2011

Out of the blue, early on the morning of May 2, while I was working out, I received a text from Brad Adamson that said that Zions was ready to fund us. I was excited to let everyone know, but he asked that I call him first to review a few specifics.

I was nodding my head in excitement as he told me they had everything ready. Then he said, "There's only a slight change. We can only do two-thirds of what we initially said."

We had come up short. I approached the majority shareholder to let him know what had happened. He reaffirmed that we needed to honor what we had committed to, which was the full amount. I understood. A commitment is a commitment.

I immediately called a meeting with the Fishbowl Captains and the other minority shareholders. I let them know what had taken place and that we were significantly short. We really had little in the bank after the challenging April. We were trying to build a little bit of cash for 2011, but we were still growing, which incurred personnel and infrastructure costs.

When I shared what we were up against—and this is one of the greatest memories I'll ever have—the people in the meeting immediately stepped forward and said, "I can get a second mortgage on my home," or "Could we use personal credit cards?" or "Wouldn't our 401(k)s be eligible for this?" Everyone was amazing in showing their willingness to find a way. For them, there was no other option except to move forward, and they were ready and willing to do everything that it took to succeed for the company.

We closed the deal on May 20 and secured a seven-year loan with Zions. We were really flying high at that point, even though we had drained our bank account again. Our confidence was strong and our energy and exuberance to build and create soared. We set an outstanding pace for an extraordinary year. In fact, in September I suggested that we could pay off the loan before the first principal payment was due.

DECEMBER 28, 2011

Part of the negotiation of the bank coming up short from what they originally had offered was that for the first six months—until December 28, 2011—the loan was interest only. The principal kicked in during the seventh month.

As that time quickly approached, I placed a call to Brad Adamson at Zions Bank and said, "You know, Brad, we have a real problem with paying the amount of principal that is due this month in our first principal payment." He's a calm person by nature, but at that point he was waiting for the floor to fall out beneath him because so many people were having problems paying loans at the time.

Not wanting to leave him in suspense too long, I continued, "We don't want to pay the first principal payment amount. We want to pay it all. Would that be okay with you?"

I could tell he was smiling as we both chuckled a bit, before discussing our plan for making Fishbowl debt free and getting its stock back. We had built a stock-option plan for our employees that we really wanted to start rolling out, but to do that we needed to repay the bank, so the stock would no longer be tied up as collateral. We talked for a while, but he didn't make us feel bad for not making much money. It was actually a great story: Two local companies had locked arms and pulled off a few miracles together, Zions by providing the loan, and Fishbowl by paying it off seven years early. They were gracious and excited that we were able to do it.

MAKING A BIG DEAL ABOUT OUR BIG DEAL

We made a big event out of it, and invited newspapers and TV stations on December 28 to see us present a big cardboard check to the CEO of Zions, Scott Anderson, and his team. That day we became debt free, and we were able to move forward next year with our stock-option plan. Fishbowl now has many new owners as a result of paying off our loan early. It did put us in a pretty tough position as far as cash flow for the next several months, but even though it was difficult to manage every penny so carefully, it was worth it. It made us frugal and humble, caused us to reevaluate all of our expenditures, and let us grow again at a brisk pace with our own cash.

Here are Mary's additions to this story:

> Now we've shared what David went through health-wise and how he found the strength to do all this. This all happened before he had his back surgery, so he was on crutches and his left leg was numb, he had kidney stones, and yet through all the tremendous pain, he got up every day and would say, "Staying in bed would kill me." I recall one day while working in our conference room that he had duct-taped a heating pad to his good leg. His other leg was completely numb and would soon require surgery. The fact that he couldn't walk without the aid of crutches never slowed him down. As a leadership team, we would often encourage him to take some time off to rest and heal. He would share that coming to Fishbowl every day helped to heal him and get him healthy because he had something to do that he believed in. Standing on crutches, surrounded by all of our employees, he shared the truth of his past

debt issues and why it was so important to pay off the loan. He shared his challenges with the steel mill and held nothing back.

In my 20 years of working with executives, I never witnessed a leader put everything on the line and believe so much in his company and employees. Fishbowl did not have adequate assets to cover the loan, so David put everything he owned up as collateral. We knew that we had to make that money for Fishbowl, but we also knew that we needed to deliver in order to return the funds to David.

David was very happy the day we paid the loan off because he could give stock to the employees and could now share the company, but the Captains and I were happy that day because it meant that we could give back all the things that were rightfully David's. That's one reason you see the joyous looks on all of our faces. And another lesson is that we saw what a CEO needs to do to protect a company, but that's what leaders and captains do to protect their CEO. You just don't say, "Oops, sorry it didn't work out, boss." It was a tremendous, noble thing to know what David had done, and we as his leadership team did what we were supposed to do. It was just not an option that David could lose everything in his service to us. He didn't want the employees to know because he didn't do it for the glory. Day in and day out, David always knew that those things would come back. The part that is extraordinary about the employees is that they never doubted, either. They believed in their product and in their company and that belief never faltered.

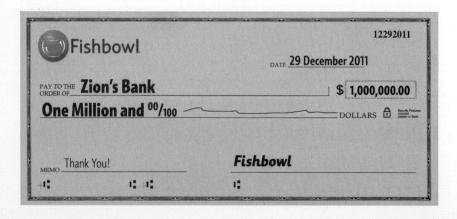

We were debt free. There were times when we literally had $10 in the bank, yet because of the way David taught and treated the employees, everyone knew that we were richer than so many other companies. We have educated our employees to know that venture capital is debt. We kept our heads above water and swam until we were debt free. We had everything we needed, and we took care of one another. We didn't waste and we didn't spend money in silos. We ate well, we made payroll, we laughed, we had fun, we were frugal and we achieved record sales. It was a time of great abundance, even with only $10 in the bank.

Fast forward to the year 2012. Paying off Zions in December 2011 drained us and actually put us in a negative position for the next couple of months. We were committed to never missing a payroll, so we'd put together a few plans just in case things went a little sideways. So we had to take out another short-term line of credit and max out our credit cards, which we had never done before. In essence, we went back into debt by about $600,000 to be able to grow and make payroll, pay taxes, and do everything we needed to do to be healthy as a company. None of our employee's benefits were affected, none of their salaries were cut, and no payrolls were missed.

As 2012 proceeded, we were able to chip away at some of these things, particularly in the last four months. By April all of our payables were back up to being current. They had never gone past due, but we'd had to stretch them out to the very last day—not what I like to do. In October we paid the credit cards off, and by December we paid the last bit of our line of credit and all of our estimated taxes for the year. We became debt free again in December 2012.

SUPPLEMENTAL MATERIALS AND EXERCISES TO DEVELOP YOUR OWN NON-NEGOTIABLES AND DEFINING ATTRIBUTES

Lessons Learned

1. Together as a team we can do anything, and it is a privilege to sacrifice.

2. To be loyal to one another and to all things Fishbowl is the glue that holds everything in the Bowl together.

3. We stand for and with one another, and our word is our bond to one another.

4. We discovered a profound peace in this unity because our word is our bond. We simply do not break it.

5. It's important to be loyal to our dreams and to the dreams of others.

6. We can be loyal to one another without agreeing with them. We can honor their choices in life.

7. Family and friends can surprise you and express loyalty when you least expect it. Be open to let life and people surprise you once in a while.

Never let your dreams die in the daylight.

Arise each day and sculpt the day purposefully like an artist, making it your own.

Fight for what you believe in.

Honor the struggle as something that is good and necessary and important in summoning and stretching the best within you.

Victory is close.

—Brendon Burchard, author of The Charge

Write down the most important lessons you learned from the Loyalty Non-Negotiable and how you can apply it in your life.

1. _____

2. _____

3. _____

4. _____

5. _____

6. _____

7. _____

The Attributes of Loyalty

1. Promises must be more than words, even if they require sacrifice.

2. Think of your organization like a family—one where you sacrifice and serve together as one, with hearts and love working for mutual success.

3. Embrace hard work. Arrive early, complete your tasks, do more than required, follow through, help others, always try to say yes—and be happy while doing it all.

4. Don't complain by stirring up underground currents. Address things properly with the appropriate people.

5. Do your job. Stick with it, especially when times get tough.

6. Always be an active proponent of your company, and be willing to support and defend it and your coworkers at all times.

COMPLETE THE FOLLOWING EXERCISES AND RETURN TO THIS SECTION TO ADD YOUR OWN NON-NEGOTIABLE AND DEFINING ATTRIBUTES

Enter your Non-Negotiable Value_____

1. _____
2. _____
3. _____
4. _____
5. _____
6. _____
7. _____

GAME TIME: PERSONAL

If you are trying to work on loyalty on a very personal basis (and thus you are concerned about privacy), this simple yet effective exercise is for you.

- Identify and list three to five traits that you feel strongly represent people who demonstrate true loyalty—traits that you highly respect and to which you aspire. None of us is perfect and we can always make improvements—that is the basis of the 7 Non-Negotiables. So circle the one on which you would most like to make progress and write it at the top of a 3 × 5 card.

- Below that, write some actions you might take to move in the direction you want to go. These are areas where you can admit to yourself you are a little weak. This part of the exercise is critical and will require you to be honest and maybe even set your pride aside. If you do this you'll see the greatest personal improvement.

- Now take that card and fold it twice so it can fit into your pocket or post it where you are going to run into it at least twice a day. The more frequently you see it, the better.

- Measure your progress in this exercise by weeks:

  - Week 1: Every time you come across this folded card, unfold it, read what you wrote, and ask yourself how you are progressing. If you do this several times a day, by the end of week 1 you will know what is on this card by heart.

  - Week 2 and beyond: You shouldn't have to read the card anymore, but each time you see it, ask yourself how you are progressing. The question is important because the more often you ask this question, the more your brain will work toward effectively solving the problem by helping you make better choices at the moment you need to make them.

- Continue this process for as long as you feel you need to make progress, or until you've reached the desired level of loyalty.

- Don't stop with one word. Continue to do this with all five words and take as much time as is necessary.

GAME TIME: INTERPERSONAL

If you are working on developing better loyalty between yourself and another individual, you can use this activity with a substantial variation at the start.

Rather than you picking the trait you want to work on, meet privately with the person with whom you want to make improvements. If they are willing to support this activity, have them pick the trait that would mean the most to them for you to work on. Have them also write down the kinds of activities you could do—or do better at—that would show them you are actively working to make progress on the trait. Do likewise for them, then trade cards.

From this point on, follow the process outlined in the personal exercise, making sure you ask the right types of questions that will allow your brain to come up with answers that improve your actions over time.

INTERPERSONAL RETROSPECTIVE

With two people, it is best to do retrospectives—ideally once a month—to learn whether each party perceives the other to be making progress. Give honest feedback without being offensive and accept it without being offended. Make the necessary adjustment and continue moving forward until you've reached the level you've agreed upon.

EXTRA CREDIT FOR CHAMPION PLAYERS

As in the personal exercise, do this with all five words and take as much time as is necessary. Continual progress in a positive direction will only make interpersonal relationships better over time, no matter how long it takes. It is well worth the effort.

GAME TIME: GROUP ACTIVITY

This exercise is designed to get you thinking about what loyalty is, learn to recognize it in others, and nurture it in yourself. Loyalty often breaks down when we sense that we have been wronged. Spending time dwelling on such negative behavior generally will cause us to spiral downward. This game is intended to interrupt the traditional patterns found in the workplace, replacing them with positive actions designed to improve loyalty among groups of interdependent people. The game is called Loyalty Bingo and it is designed to get employees focused on positive behaviors around us that demonstrate loyalty, the concept being that we are what we focus on.

B	I	N	G	O
Unwavering Commitment	Sincere in Word and Action	Understanding	Helpful	Service to Others
Supportive	Sense of Duty	Integrity	Faithful	Problem Solver
Honor	Sense of Humor	**FREE SPACE**	Maintains Confidence	Selflessness
Devoted to the Cause	Willing to Sacrifice	Respects Others	Expresses Gratitude	Follows Directions
Innovative	Fulfills Obligations	Reliable	Trust	Pleasant to Work with

Rules for Loyalty Bingo

1. Discuss with your group the traits or characteristics of loyalty the team thinks would be important in their work environment. Use these to populate your Bingo sheet. We've provided this sheet as an example. Feel free to replace any terms you like. What's most

important is that the team agrees these are traits they think are important.

2. Distribute the Bingo cards to your team, then turn them loose to identify the people they interact with daily who demonstrate these characteristics. Players put the name of the person below the characteristic and then write a short paragraph about how this person demonstrates that trait. Three or more sentences are good enough, but they must document why that person's name is assigned to the space. This will become important in the retrospective later.

3. Determine the rules of the game. You might play traditional Bingo where you are working to get the same name across five spots, or you can play whiteout and the first person to completely fill the card wins. It is important to offer a prize to the winner. You should also plan on two or three prizes for the people whose names are mentioned most. This combination will create the proper incentive for participation by demonstrating the traits of loyalty as the team has defined them.

4. This exercise can be repeated as many times as needed to create the desired environment and behavioral traits you believe will result in the Hard Results your business is seeking.

TEAM RETROSPECTIVES

At the end of each game, pull the participants together and discuss what they've seen and what impact the game has had on improving Soft Traits related to loyalty. Discuss some of the short paragraphs highlighting employees, calling attention to those traits you feel will be most important to your organization going forward. In your retrospective, end with prizes for the winner and the people who have had their names documented the most. Make sure the prizes have perceived value, so each time you repeat the exercise you get the level of participation you are after.

There will come a time when you will want to share with everyone that the real purpose of the activity is to have people focus on positive traits rather than negative behavior. Make sure they understand that individuals and groups gravitate toward those things that they focus on most. If they focus on negative issues, they will become more negative over time. If they focus their attention on positive issues, their behavior will start to reflect those issues they discuss and focus on most. As these Soft Traits become more ingrained, Hard Results will follow in all areas of the business and their personal lives.

EXTRA CREDIT FOR CHAMPION PLAYERS

Without warning, pick someone who has engaged more fully than the rest of the group. He or she might not be the same person who is getting all the recognition on the Bingo sheet, but go out of your way to publicly express your appreciation for his or her support of the exercise. This might include giving them one of the planned prizes. Repeat this as needed to keep the energy high and participation at a level that will ensure the activity is successful. It will also demonstrate your loyalty to the players who support your initiative to change.

5

COMMITMENT

REFLECT on the Attributes of the Non-Negotiable to Develop Your Soft Traits

LEARN from the Failing Up Chronicles and Create Your Hard Results

DISCOVER Opportunities Earned

If you could kick the person in the pants responsible for most of your trouble, you wouldn't sit for a month.

—Theodore Roosevelt

REFLECTING ON THE ATTRIBUTES OF THE NON-NEGOTIABLE: THE MEANING OF FAILING UP

As we make and keep commitments, even small ones, we establish an inner integrity that gives us the self-control, courage, and strength to accept responsibility for our lives. Commitment begins with becoming accountable.

One of my first humbling experiences came early in my life, when I learned the value of commitment by failing in some important areas. It taught me that I was capable of achieving a measure of success on my own, but that nothing compares to winning as a team. So many leaders work hard and have good intentions but still find themselves alone.

This is my story of standing alone on the mountain of regret and how I discovered the courage to face it and change what I valued in life. The metrics are simple for this Non-Negotiable: Commitment is an all-or-nothing game.

FAILING UP CHRONICLES: WINNING, LOSING, AND LEARNING THE TRUE MEANING OF COMMITMENT

My three summers as a salesman taught me lessons not only in perseverance in the face of adversity, but also in the importance of lifting others and making sure everyone succeeds together. That is what leadership is all about.

SUMMER 1981: FLYING LESSONS WITH THE EAGLE MARKETING CORPORATION

I was 22 in the summer of 1981. I was newly married and my first child, Amber, had been born the previous October. I needed a job in order to continue attending Brigham Young University and to support my family. I had arranged a summer job with friends, but unfortunately it fell through at the last moment and I was desperate to find something to replace it.

Then a classified ad in a local newspaper caught my eye. It assured me that if I'd like to make a lot of money for the summer, I only needed to come and watch a presentation that Saturday. I was intrigued; I definitely needed the money, so I made arrangements with a few other people to watch the presentation.

The job was to go out and sell books door to door. I recall the presenters had a little film projector that they manually turned frame by frame. The film showed guys selling books; they were happy, driving nice cars, and holding fistfuls of money. My wife was with me and as soon as we left the meeting, she said, "There's no way we're going to do that. There's no guarantee, no nothing."

Despite her valid concerns, I decided I wanted to try selling. I felt like I could do it, I knew I could work hard, and from what they said it sounded like all I needed to do was knock on enough doors and I could make money. I guess I was naïve enough to believe that, and so I said yes and committed to go out and sell books.

So, at the ripe age of 22, after convincing my wife that we wouldn't starve, I began my first official summer job, working for a company called Eagle Marketing and selling character-building books and illustrated religious books with cassette tapes door to door. It was grueling work. It took a lot of perseverance to knock on enough doors and sell enough products to make the summer job profitable while paying our own expenses.

For the first year, I was assigned to the Dallas/Fort Worth area with a team of six people. We set out on our adventure right after school let out in May 1981. By the end of two weeks, all the other team members had given up and quit except my manager, who decided he wanted to have a vacation in Texas.

I might have packed up and gone home, too, except I didn't have enough money to return to Utah and I had promised my wife I would be successful. I connected with a local church and a nice lady rented a spare room to my family. I had just enough money to cover the rent and buy a few groceries.

The way I looked at my situation was that I now had all this territory in Dallas, Fort Worth, and Arlington that I didn't have to share with anybody. I could sell a ton of books! I didn't think about the team dynamic. I had never done it before, so I didn't know what I didn't know, which looking back on that time was a great philosophy to have.

I dug in and worked hard. As a result of my dedication, something extraordinary happened: I became the top salesperson for the company, breaking all their sales records by a factor of four. It was so far beyond what any previous salesperson had achieved that it seemed almost unbelievable, both to the company and to me. My secret to succeeding as an individual was hard work, plain and simple.

When I returned to Utah after completing the summer job, I was excited to "get the big check" because it was my only frame of reference for measuring success at the time. Both the president, Steve Shallenberger, and the vice president, Rod Mann, congratulated me, and then reviewed all my contracts to make sure they were all accurate because the numbers were so high.

It was a great summer for a young, inexperienced kid of 22. I discovered that I had some useful skills: I could sell, and I knew how to work hard. I worked relentlessly. I had tasted business and financial success, and it stuck in my mind that I could achieve great things and earn a great income if I just believed in myself and put every fiber of my heart and mind into my efforts.

SUMMER 1982: FAILING BIG AT WHAT REALLY MATTERS, AND DISCOVERING THE TRUE MEANING OF COMMITMENT

The next year, I was invited back to serve as the manager of a team. I didn't get a lot of training on how to be a manager. My job was just to recruit as many people as I could, bring them to the area we had been assigned, and try to make a lot of sales. My confidence was still as high as it was the summer before, even more so. I simply believed that if I found good guys, then they would all do what I did. . . .

I recruited 12 sales reps, the biggest team in the history of the company to that point. One of them was my brother-in-law. How could I go wrong? I thought, *This is going to be great. We'll go out and have an incredible summer, break all the team and individual records. All these salespeople are going to be terrific. This will be a lot of fun and we will score big again.*

We were assigned to Los Angeles and we headed out with bravado and gusto. However, after two weeks most of the salesmen had failed to make a sale. During that weekly meeting, everyone was complaining loudly about how we had been allocated such a crummy territory and that no one was listening to them or buying the books.

I thought back on the previous summer and proudly told them, "I had no team and no manager to help me. Why don't you guys just go out and work and quit bellyaching? If you guys can't go out and work hard, then why don't you just go home?"

Within the next two weeks every one of them had gone home.

I was left alone, just like the previous year. Only this time, it felt like a lead weight in my stomach. I was the team leader, and the owners believed in me and trusted me. All the hard work in the world wasn't going to change the fact that I had lost my team. I had failed at what was most important and I could feel it in every part of my being.

I had worked so hard for four months to recruit these guys. I did the best that I could to prepare them. We'd had several team meetings prior to going out in the summer, yet lo and behold I was by myself again. Even my brother-in-law quit—can you imagine that? Looking back, I can't blame him or anyone else.

I remember driving alone on the Antelope Valley Freeway in California. It was about an hour's drive to the area where I was selling, and I remember specifically thinking as I drove, *I feel horrible. I'm still the top salesperson in the company, but I'm probably the worst manager in the history of the company.* I was embarrassed, broken, and in pain. It was in that moment that I realized that fulfillment came from helping others succeed and that my own self-gratification of being the top salesperson again was hollow. There was no comparison. I vowed to accept my situation, take accountability for it, and finish the summer strong because I had no other option. Most important, though, I vowed to do things differently the next year.

I have nothing to offer but blood, toil, tears, and sweat.

—*Winston Churchill*

Summer 1983: Building a Legacy, Not Just a Fortune, by Serving

The following summer, I was 24 years old and now had two children. Leaving my previous record for the biggest team in the dust, I recruited 32 people this time around. I came up with a plan to spend all my time with each of my teammates, and none selling on my own. I was going to dedicate every moment to my team's success. I also didn't want to compete with my own teammates, which removed a massive conflict of interest in my mind.

I spent the entire summer driving to different cities to work with them, going out and knocking on doors all day long. The only sleep I got was on their apartment floors or sofas. The result of my efforts was amazing. All but one of my teammates stayed the entire summer. The one person who returned home because of an illness would have stayed because he, too, was succeeding.

There were a total of 300 people in the company selling at the time. Of the top 25 salespeople for that summer, 22 were members of my team. My success came from helping them to be successful. They sensed my dedication to their success because they saw that I was willing to sacrifice my personal sales for theirs. I turned all the sales over to the team, and we all won in the end. They became great managers and I was eventually made an executive of the company.

My shift from thinking only of myself to helping others succeed had a lasting impact on me, even today at age 54. Although our exact sales numbers escape me, I still remember how I felt. Seeing the difference between the summers of 1982 and 1983 was one of my greatest learning experiences. I learned that it is essential for leaders to demonstrate, day in and day out, that they are committed to helping those who they lead to succeed. I reversed my whole way of thinking from "If you can't make it, go home," to "There is absolutely no way you're going home. I've got your back. We'll find a way to be successful together." By shifting my focus from my own interests, glory, and gratification in order to help others become successful, I helped us all to achieve more than any of us could have done by ourselves. When we work as a team, no one should be left behind.

In fact, our success story was so dramatic that the rest of the company competed against our team in a sales challenge. It was 320 people against our little team of 32, and we still outsold them. That's how powerful this management style turned out to be.

I've worked too hard to quit now.

—*Michael Jordan*

REFLECTING ON LESSONS LEARNED

To become great at your job, you need people around you with the wisdom to see your hidden potential. I worked for two great men who saw potential in me and didn't fire me when I so obviously failed. I lost my entire team and demonstrated that I was a horrible leader, terrible manager, and not much of a friend because I had treated my people like they were a nuisance. But Steve and Rod were willing to let me fail, learn from it, and bounce higher. They saw in me a person who could Fail Up—to learn from my mistakes and do better in the future—and I was fortunate to be in an environment that allowed me to do so.

Driving up Antelope Valley Freeway in the summer of 1982, I felt so sad at the fact that my teammates had left and that I had failed them, I wanted to steer off the side of the road and crash to hide my shame. Yet a spirit swelled up inside of me and said, "I know how to do things in a different way. I trust that there is a better way to lead, and that is to dedicate myself to the team."

Having an all-or-nothing type of personality, I had to give my entire self to my team, and I needed to recruit enough people to make sure it was worth it for everyone. I calculated that to create financial success for the company, I would have to give up selling and create a team large enough to achieve a financial win for me as their leader. But the key point is that before achieving these Hard Results, I had to adjust my Soft Traits. I had to become more patient, tolerant, and committed to others. I had to learn how to serve, teach, and mentor while continuing to deliver strong results. I had to go out and show them that I could close and that they could, too.

There's a lesson to be learned here: You can be a catalyst for change. I was the one who conceived the idea of serving others by going out and selling with them, but I soon found that my example also inspired my colleagues to help their own teammates succeed. Every week I would go to an apartment and work exclusively with the young men who were living there. After a few weeks of doing this, I learned that those I had taught would go out in pairs and help each other. If somebody was struggling with sales, one of the stronger sales-people would let him sell with him in his area, or he would go into that person's area and help him close some deals. Becoming a leader by committing to serving others turned out to be a contagious principle.

Applying Commitment

Picture a teeter-totter with a fulcrum in the middle. As you move the fulcrum toward an object, you can lift more. You have greater lever-age. The role of an individual as a leader is to move the fulcrum in the right direction so that the units of output increase even as the units of input remain the same. If the fulcrum stays in the middle, it's always one for one. You get exactly what you put in. But if you move the fulcrum away from you, you have greater leverage so that one unit of input has multiple units of output.

This example shows that when a person allocates himself as a resource to others as a servant leader, he can get more out of his team's efforts by moving the fulcrum of effort. Leaders must be committed in word and in deed. They must be consistent, and their efforts can't be short-lived. People will naturally work harder for you when they see you are personally interested in them at a deep level, and that you don't ever give up trying to help them be better at whatever they're doing.

Granted, some employees may not be fully skilled, or may have issues outside the workplace that they need your help with. But if people see you are genuinely interested in them as individuals, they'll exceed your expectations—and often their own.

Deploying Commitment

One of the biggest hurdles to commitment is fear of rejection—fear of losing. If you can embrace the concept of Failing Up, this fear melts away. I have faced losing Fishbowl many times, but I loved the people so much that I was willing to place everything I had on the line for them. More important, I was willing to do so with joy in my heart. As a result, there were also many times at Fishbowl where I have felt my care and commitment returned.

When my son, Cam, was ill, I did not set foot in the office for six months, as he required constant care. I remained connected via e-mail, but the team did all the heavy lifting while offering tremendous support to me and my family. Cam was one of Fishbowl's first hires, and his legacy lives on in so many ways. Their commitment to Cam's memory and contribution can be seen and felt throughout the entire building. You can commit to changing your life for the better, just as my son and I have done.

In Your Personal Life

In the summer of 1982, even though I was the top salesperson again and actually outperformed the previous summer, I felt very empty. A true principle of life and leadership is that if you attempt to gain all the glory and win all the awards while leaving others to suffer along the way, neither your glory nor your happiness will last for long.

The summer of 1983 was a completely different story. I wasn't yet aware of the phrase "being in the people business," but I was living it by making sure that everyone on my team was able to be as successful as possible. My attitude made all the difference in creating results that were completely opposite from what took place the summer before, when everyone left. I didn't think about the money; I just trusted in the principle of making sure nobody went home. If nobody went home, then I knew I had inspired them to work hard enough to sell. And if they sold, with my help—and the help of great performers on the team—they could positively influence their coworkers. That plan yielded long-term dividends. I've bumped into these guys in later years and they still bring up what that summer meant to them and how it changed their lives through the ways that they think about business and leadership. There's an everlasting bond.

I have so much gratitude for the winning and failing I experienced 30 years ago. I will feel joyful about that experience the rest of my life because I had a positive effect on those people and they had a positive effect on me. We became an all-star team. A bond forms when you serve one another and never give up on one another, one that lasts your entire life. That's the type of commitment to people that we need to make in our youth. It lets us hold our heads high and not feel afraid to greet the people we bonded with when we see them years later, because we know we did our very best on their behalf.

BUSINESS APPLICATIONS OF DEPLOYING COMMITMENT

Likewise, as our employees at Fishbowl realize my commitment to them, they are willing to do extraordinary things for the company and for me as a leader. And it can be the same at your company, too. I spend at least half of my time with the top 20 percent performers in my organization rather than focusing on the 80 percent who generally produce around 20 percent of the results. Focusing this way on the top performers has an interesting effect: They consistently increase their output, which naturally elevates everyone else. Most top performers who are firmly committed will be eager to help others on the team achieve their goals. I believe that someone who is not performing well but who is committed will do well in time. My door and my e-mail are always open to the 80 percent as they commit to improving themselves.

Often the top performers are left on their own and are not fully appreciated because they're doing great. We have a tendency to focus on the weakest links and try to uplift them, which usually takes up all of our bandwidth and energy. My recommendation is to spend at least half of your time with the top performers. Everyone will benefit in the long run.

My suggestion for anyone looking for a place to grow a career and expand their opportunities is to look for the type of culture, leaders, and environment that will allow you to come in and do your best while failing from time to time. I don't mean that you should deliberately do poorly and fail. Instead, I encourage you to trust that when you make mistakes, there will be people there to pick you up and point you in the right direction. Don't be afraid to work hard. Seek out people who will give you feedback about your blind spots. From your self-examination you'll be able to see your flaws clearly and grow beyond them day by day.

I would challenge every leader to give your people—who have entrusted their careers to you, and to whom you have entrusted your company's resources—the latitude to innovate. Let them experiment in new areas from time to time so that they can be tested and increase their confidence, competence, and capacity. And even if they fail in some of their endeavors, great lessons can come from failure.

The greatest lesson I learned from the summer of 1982 was that I needed to serve the people I led. I didn't understand this principle at that time. I thought I could just sell, lead, and instruct and that would be enough. I had no idea that I had to get involved, roll up my sleeves, and spend all my time with them so that they would feel comfortable with me and see that I really did care. As leaders, we need to show our people that we are willing to lock arms and walk out with them—that whether it rains or snows or is sunny, we will be there no matter what.

INNOVATIVE COMPENSATION AND BENEFIT PROGRAMS

Building a company designed to last for 100-plus years starts with implementing a fair compensation program for employees. At Fishbowl, because every employee contributes to sales, every member of the company receives a commission (as opposed to emphasizing a profit share or bonus). The ratios vary across departments, and are based on the metrics the individuals are most able to directly control, but everyone has skin in the game, which affects our overall revenue.

Benefits of Fishbowl's Compensation Plan

- Every employee is inherently motivated to help the company focus on creating revenue.

- Job security and company stability increase, as the company's greatest cost—payroll—rises and falls automatically along with revenue creation.

- It closes the inherent gaps and divisions between departments by ensuring everyone is focused on revenue, profit, and savings versus individual department agendas.

The commission structure supports the Non-Negotiable of commitment by encouraging transparency and team participation. Everyone knows what the monthly operational costs are. Each day the employees receive a report on how much revenue is needed to meet and surpass that number. Two-thirds of the revenue beyond the break-even sum goes to the commission pools for each department to share among its members. The other third goes to the company.

Our employees support this structure, which has made it easier for potential stars to achieve their financial goals. We seldom need to change a base salary. Individuals who are ready for an increase are ready to build, sell, train, and support to a greater degree (in other words, to produce more revenue). This means that the rise in income is something our team members can largely influence and control on their own.

We also provide our employees with a rich benefit and 401(k) program (which matches at 10 percent) and numerous individual and family enrichment programs that promote health and the opportunity to develop personally and professionally.

STARTING YOUR OWN BUSINESS

When I meet people, many of whom are pondering their futures as so many millions of Americans have been doing since the recession, I see a common theme in every one of their faces, whether they are employed, seeking employment, or considering a business idea of their own. Regardless of the circumstances, the question I see in their eyes and hear in their voices is invariably, "What about the risk?"

In every direction they see uncertainty, fear, trepidation, and, yes, substantial risk. "Am I working for the right company? Could I be working for a better company? Would I be able to succeed if I started a company of my own, and would I be glad I'd moved forward?"

Starting a business is certainly not for everyone. Some people worry that others will view them as a loser if they try out a business, or a project, or a skill, and that it will cost them their credibility. They fear it will be far more difficult to find another opportunity or job after a business or a project failure, because others will question their competence or even their worth.

The reality can be different if you are open to the possibility that when you are willing to put your whole self on the line for a new project, to test an idea, or to take a shot at creating a better and happier life, you are making the most courageous choice of your life. When you look at it from this perspective, you will also be open to the possibility that many people will ultimately respect your choice, even if (and especially if) you should fail. You might also inspire others to discover their own courage to try something new and get out of their comfort zone.

Don't live a life full of regrets. It's so much more fulfilling to be able to look back on a life full of growth and mistakes than it is to look back on one full of safety and missed opportunities. I couldn't live with myself if I wasn't willing to go out on a limb and take calculated risks every day. That's what living is all about. Anything else is unsatisfying and not worth your time.

Every day I guide our Fishbowl team to Fail Up and embrace our failures. We celebrate and honor the opportunity to move forward with full force, knowing that mistakes are some of the most essential steps in the process. It is our mistakes that present us with incomparable opportunities to grow and to learn.

The vast majority of successful business owners have failed multiple times before they found outstanding success. I am no exception. Neither are most of the tremendous executives I work with, both within and outside our company walls.

As to the statement that true entrepreneurs are rabidly risk averse: Yes, there is some truth to that fact. Here's how that principle is working for us.

We manage our company's risk by operating on a cash basis. We are debt free. We only buy what we can pay for. Because we avoid debt, we don't incur the level of financial risk that other companies might. We pay our bills immediately. By going home each day with all bills paid and no debt, I am able to rest more easily. If conditions were to change, I would be solid, knowing that we could last for 60 more days without needing to pay further bills.

Our compensation method also eases Fishbowl's risk. Because everyone in the company is paid a base amount plus commission, the costs associated with payroll are able to slide up and down organically. This provides a natural protection for both the company's financial position and the employees' level of assurance about keeping their jobs.

We also manage with complete transparency. Everybody knows fully and accurately where the company stands. This full disclosure and knowledge helps to alleviate fears and educates employees on how to run a business, as well as how to manage their personal and family finances with skill.

Debt and venture capital have supported the big wins of any number of flash-in-the-pan ideas, but by forgoing both we have created a company that will be around for future generations with the same guiding principles in place today.

Similarly, we control the quality of our product by developing our software and supporting our product in house. Yes, outsourcing development and customer support may be more economical in the short term—but the quality of the product we deliver by creating and supporting the product ourselves provides sustainability that well outweighs the additional cost. We pay less to operate our business as the quality of our product increases.

Is running a business risky? Does trying out a new idea or developing a new skill expose your vulnerabilities to others? Yes and yes. What if you fail? Inevitably, at least some of the time, you will. Yet this is a requisite step that will allow you to grow and progress.

We need to learn to treasure and even celebrate our inevitable failures. And yes, after having done everything in our power to prepare, to organize, and to remove the obstacles of debt, doubt, fear, and ego, we must also learn to celebrate risk. Why? Because the willingness to venture forward, to expose our vulnerabilities, to show our courage, and even to fail is the only thing that can protect us from the biggest danger of all—the risk and pain of regret.

So what's stopping you from starting a business (or reinventing your current job) right now?

SUPPLEMENTAL MATERIALS AND EXERCISES TO DEVELOP YOUR OWN NON-NEGOTIABLES AND DEFINING ATTRIBUTES

> Write down the most important lessons you learned from the Commitment Non-Negotiable and how you can apply it in your life.
>
> 1. _____
> 2. _____
> 3. _____
> 4. _____
> 5. _____
> 6. _____
> 7. _____

The Attributes of Commitment

1. Hold nothing back and work like this is your last job.

2. Whatever your work is, make it your number one priority. Find something that compels you to want to be in it for the long haul.

3. Commit to growth for yourself and others.

4. Know that someone is truly committed to their company when they first accept, then improve upon, the corporate culture.

5. Build relationships. Know people's names. Make friends. Serve others. Say hello. Value people above all else. Do something to make your team happy. Create positive feelings that people can take home and share with their families.

6. Transcend the exchange of time for money, autonomy, or accountability.

7. Adopt and improve the organization's vision and culture, and see it carefully through to the next generation.

COMPLETE THE FOLLOWING EXERCISES AND RETURN TO THIS SECTION TO ADD YOUR OWN NON-NEGOTIABLE AND DEFINING ATTRIBUTES

Enter your Non-Negotiable Value_____

1. _____

2. _____

3. _____

4. _____

5. _____

6. _____

7. _____

Commitment is a vital component of success in all aspects of life, both professionally and personally. Small hurdles can lead to feelings of inadequacy when confronting the bigger picture, and can hinder one's ability not only to fully commit but also to progress and take on newer and potentially more exciting opportunities. Finding ways to overcome the small hurdles can benefit everyone in their individual goals, their interpersonal communications, and their successful work within or as leader of a group.

Furthermore, it is important to recognize that individuals commit themselves in their own unique ways, and we should never judge others' choices of how they have decided to dedicate themselves. As a person who has made some off-the-beaten-path decisions, I find it important for others to understand that these decisions were not made on an ad hoc basis, but rather were the result of much thought and consideration. If we can all manage to respect the decisions and commitments of those around us, we will be in a better position to support one another in those commitments.

On a personal level, learning how to identify the hurdles that were impeding me has allowed me to achieve a much higher level of commitment both at work and with family and friends. I recognized that committing to a concept or big picture is just the first step. The next is to embrace what is going to be required of me so I can live up to that commitment and figure out the barriers that might trip me up.

Being asked to lead at Fishbowl was an easy big-picture commitment for me. The team was composed of honest, good people working toward a goal I could easily get behind. When the hurdles appeared, I had to become a stronger leader and individual and learn to express myself as such. I had to learn to give tough news and not back down. I had to learn to say no. My first step toward becoming fully committed was to start by meeting with each member of the team individually to earn their respect and get comfortable stating my views to them. It was an effective way for me to become better at speaking to the group as a whole while still listening and taking great advice, and I was able to stay committed to the job that was asked of me.

In this way, the purpose of this exercise is to determine what you are truly committed to, and to identify hurdles that are keeping you from becoming fully committed.

1. Write down one part of your life where you feel deeply committed but where you have struggled to feel capable of truly achieving things.

2. List the specific aspect(s) of this task/duty/responsibility preventing you from moving forward and fully committing.

3. Choose one of these hurdles and determine why you struggle with it. Is it something you disagree with and feel uncomfortable addressing? Does it involve dealing with an individual whom you find difficult? Does it require you to do something that you find difficult?

4. List five things that you can do to overcome or remove this hurdle. Spend one week actively pursuing these actions. Determine a method of reminding yourself on a daily basis to do so.

5. Once the week is up, move on to the next hurdle and repeat the previous steps, with the goal of removing all of your hurdles to success and commitment.

TEAM SUPPORT AND ACCOUNTABILITY RETROSPECTIVE

This exercise can be done individually or as a group. If done as a group, gather everyone together once a month to review and share their successes and struggles. This helps us learn how better to deal with these hurdles to commitment, and to reevaluate both what we have committed to and the seriousness of the hurdles we seek to overcome. A group setting is a perfect place to receive input on alternative means to achieve our goals.

EXTRA CREDIT FOR CHAMPION PLAYERS

Once you can look at any issue and know that you have resolved the hurdles that stand in the way of full commitment, select the next issue in your life causing you difficulty in commitment and run through the exercise again. Take a minute to realize that everyone faces these types of issues, and that working through them in a careful and kind manner is an effective way to lead a happier and more committed life, in whatever form that may take. In this way, everyone who at least tries is a champion and deserves extra credit.

6

COURAGE

REFLECT on the Attributes of the Non-Negotiable to Develop your Soft Traits

LEARN from the Failing Up Chronicles and Create Your Hard Results

DISCOVER Opportunities Earned

Courage is not having the strength to go on; it is going on when you don't have the strength.

—Theodore Roosevelt

REFLECTING ON THE ATTRIBUTES OF THE NON-NEGOTIABLE: TACKLING FEAR

One of the biggest impediments to implementing the Non-Negotiables is fear. Fear lives in a place in us where negative thoughts and feelings develop and self-defeating behaviors take root. Life is too precious to view through the filter of fear. All we need is a process that shows us how to move beyond our fears in spite of them.

Let's be honest, there is no such thing as being fearless. Life is going to present us with trials and challenges. To overcome them, we focus at Fishbowl on surrounding one another with the 7 Non-Negotiables and tackling together whatever comes our way. This makes the process much simpler, and as I have stated, the far side of complexity is simplicity.

Do we make mistakes? Yes—but instead of beating ourselves down, we reach up and discover what we can learn. Some of our best discoveries in the Bowl started out as mistakes.

Do we sometimes scare one another? Do our customers scare us? Yes, sometimes. We take a deep breath and try to keep the issue the issue. Winston Churchill's advice—"Courage is what it takes to stand up and speak; courage is also what it takes to sit down and listen"—is a great reminder to us all to seek to understand. It is also one of the best methods for overcoming fear. In seeking first to understand and not judge, this gives us an opportunity to put some time between the stimulus and the response. Taking a breather is always a good idea when we feel fearful.

Do we have disagreements? Yes. But there is only one place we can solve them—the space between right and wrong (where there is no judgment)—and that's where our greatest work is accomplished. We are on the same team; we move to the same side of the table and tackle the issue together. That makes us courageous and smart.

Fear is one of the greatest sources of stress and one of our greatest teachers. The intuitive/inventive part of our mind is difficult to nurture, and we can only access it when we are relaxed. An employee who feels supported and appreciated is more willing to devote their full energy, creativity, and passion (heart and mind) to their work, the company, and its goals, and will naturally innovate in every area within their influence. Employees who are afraid of something or someone in the organization will naturally close up to protect themselves and stop performing at their full capacity.

What can we do to help employees feel courageous enough to innovate?

1. *Leaders must have the courage to trust their people.* Specifically, leaders who truly trust their people (and the operative term is "people"—not "employees" or "human resources") know that they already have the power they need within them, and trust them to use it honorably and well. They must also trust their people to care about each other and about their customers. But first, leaders must display the courage to truly delegate authority and stewardship to their people and let them run the distance. This doesn't mean abandoning them; it means showing high courage and confidence in your people and letting them know that you are always available as a resource.

2. *People first and policies second.* We are in the people business—or we should be. Consider the statement, "Every action is consistent with specific value behaviors." At Fishbowl, our principles are our 7 Non-Negotiables of Winning: Respect, Belief, Trust, Loyalty, Commitment, Courage, and Gratitude. By following these principles instead of rigid policies, employees are empowered to make quick decisions that improve their performance—without relying on manager oversight or performance appraisals. They can adapt to changing conditions on the fly, developing their own solutions rather than worrying about policies and procedures. They are no longer paralyzed by the fear of making a mistake.

3. *We must empower employees to Fail Up.* A scared employee can never truly trust themselves or their ideas. But by developing an environment of trust, individuals and teams learn to thrive on the opportunity to try. When you truly empower them by removing their fear of failure, they will display courage without even knowing they are being courageous. Let them make some small mistakes—and a big one here and there—and they will learn,

gain confidence, and become amazing as their capacity and competencies expand. Courageous leaders value the resulting chance
to let their employees make a mistake, and these mistakes often
generate positive outcomes. Even though some outcomes will be
negative, the courage, confidence, and learning you'll provide to
your people and your company are well worth it.

4. *Open communication is critical* to putting these steps into effect.
   Two of the first things an organization loses in a fearful environment are vital and open feedback, and communication at every
   level. Courage cannot be displayed when things are going well
   and everyone loves each other, but rather when times are tough.
   The courage to confront critical issues and keep them in focus is
   essential for maintaining a fearless environment. No person and
   no entity is completely fearless. We all get a little knot in our
   guts, or have beads of sweat form on our brows, but if our environment is healthy, they are just distractions.

5. To overcome them, we must always be open regardless of the circumstances. If you, as a leader, worker, team member, or home-
   maker, have a closed-door policy, then your courage and that of
   your colleagues will be displaced by fear—courage and fear cannot mutually coexist.

Fear runs rampant in organizations today. Employees are unwill-
ing to share because they are afraid somebody will kill the messenger
or target the person who is actually trying. This causes communication to become shallow or disappear altogether. An organization that
doesn't have this healthy feedback loop can no longer discern where
to focus their problem-solving efforts—and they will likely lose all
innovative energy.

We must move away from work environments based on command
and control. We can eliminate fear when we face it head-on and create an open dialogue that separates the issue at hand from the fear it
generates. Keep the issue the issue; don't make it personal. Make sure
everyone is on the same side of the table and attack the issue together.

Our motto at Fishbowl is always: "Attack the problem, not the
individual." Only then can innovation truly occur.

CAM'S STORY

The world breaks every one and afterward many are strong at the broken places.

—*Ernest Hemingway,* A Farewell to Arms

Cameron at Brigham Young University, enjoying intramural soccer just months before he was diagnosed with gastric cancer.

Autumn in Utah is breathtaking. Our mountains transform right before our eyes as the leaves turn from the deepest green to bursts of orange and red. It was on one of those glorious autumn days that my son, Cameron, began the fight of his life—one that he would ultimately lose.

Yet from a larger perspective, I know that Cam lives on here and beyond. His legacy shapes my life and Fishbowl's every day.

Of all the challenges I've had to overcome in my life, none comes close to the loss of my son. To this day, five years later, it is still something that's incredibly difficult to share or write about. When great challenges or tragedies arrive on our doorstep, we have to just keep moving forward as best as we can. Fish that stop swimming die. Many books recommend that we pause, evaluate, and reflect, but this approach would not have worked for me. I knew then—and I know now—that if I had stopped, I would never have started again.

When I pause to remember this time in my life, I have to ask myself: Did I handle it well? Did I do the right thing? Well, I did the only thing that I could. I learned, tried, and increased in courage a little bit every day to discover, truly discover, because Western medicine had sent us home to die, how to help my son fight and to remain upbeat, positive, hopeful, faith-filled, and most of all, *courageous*.

You may be wondering, why I would share this story in a business book? I tell it because no matter what industry or company we work for, we are *all* in the people business. And none of us can ever be entirely aware of what a coworker or associate is going through in other aspects of their lives.

After Cam passed, people encouraged me to work to "get over it"; to heal and become "happy" again. But I was forever changed by this experience—and there is no going back. I will never be the same again. I will always carry the loss of my son with me. And because I knew this would be the case, I chose—with Fishbowl's help—to create a living legacy to him. I know that is how he would have wanted to be remembered, and I honor his wishes.

It's tough to maintain a sense of trust when life hands you something that shatters that trust. I climb the mountain of life differently now than I did in my younger days. I remember the law of motion—and I keep going because if I stop, there is no guarantee I would ever begin again.

JOINING THE FISHBOWL FAMILY

When I came to Fishbowl in 2004, Cam had been home for about six months from a two-year service mission to Italy. I knew early on that I needed people who I could trust and who had the courage to start turning the company around. My daughter, Lindsey, was the first person I hired, despite the fact that she had just finished high school. I knew she had organizational skills and enough confidence to help me. She had always been able to make difficult situations manageable. I also knew that Lindsey had the emotional IQ to deal with older adults. Her maturity gave me the confidence to turn that chaotic, unorganized environment over to her to correct, which she did in a short period of time.

I also began talking to Cam about possibly joining the team. He had a good job as an Italian translator, and I didn't necessarily want him to leave a well-paying job while he was still in school. But I also needed his presence, his participation, and his great 21-year-old's wisdom. So eventually I asked him to join Fishbowl—to trade his secure job for the risk of coming to work with his dad. He was Fishbowl's ninth employee and the third one I hired.

He quickly became the all-purpose man and go-to guy who figured everything out. We didn't have a marketing department or any type of Web analytics or Google expertise. We also lacked any official-looking company collateral like marketing material or product packaging. But Cam worked together with our small Fishbowl team and created something professional we could send to future customers.

Cam designed our marketing material from brochures and envelopes to letterhead and logos, learning how to do so on his own, on the fly—unflinching, courageous, and undaunted. He had no experience but he was willing to learn—and always produced beautiful products. He was the one who started us using Google and Yahoo! Pay Per Click. He figured out how to use keywords and phrases that the search engines were looking for—and he essentially put us on the map online. He knew, even back then, how crucial it was to get on Google's good side by using organic search terms and phrases.

I'll admit that even I didn't understand at the time what he meant about getting organic leads—those you didn't have to pay for. But Cam figured out how to do that all on his own. I give him a great deal of credit for being a pioneer in so many of the areas where no one else at Fishbowl had any expertise—and while he didn't have it either, he did have the courage to learn and try, fail, then try again.

Cam was fearless in his desire to contribute to the company and figure things out—so much that he always worked more than he needed to each day. Because he was also attending school full time, he would leave for classes a couple hours here and there; however, he always put in a full week of work, whether it was late at night or early in the morning. He never wanted to be a part-timer; he always wanted to be a full-time student and a full-time employee. It wasn't about the money—he just knew he could contribute, and he did.

He was a pioneer and a trailblazer, and as I look back through the lens of our 7 Non-Negotiables, I see now how he was displaying each one fully, all of the time. He had great respect for the people who had joined the company before him, despite the fact that he was doing a lot of things that they couldn't—or wouldn't—do. He believed in our product, and he learned it well enough to become a fantastic salesman for it.

Cam's fearlessness and devotion to the company was contagious. He trusted that the results of this type of work would be revealed, and we would be able to benefit from his investment. He encouraged us all to take this approach despite the fact that we'd have to spend most of our money—which wasn't very much at the time—expanding our website and improving its look and feel for our customers' first experience or "touch." It was important to us to have what we called a "high-touch" experience, even though we were essentially just a startup.

Cam's loyalty was unmatched. I don't remember him ever missing a day of work; he never wanted to. He would take his vacations on days he had tests at school, or he wouldn't use them. He was consistently committed to every aspect of his work, and he was happy and loving to people while doing it. He managed to strike a balance between maintaining focus and giving his colleagues all the time in the world if they needed it. Cam demanded that same level of commitment from everyone at Fishbowl. He remained joyful while keeping his head down and making sure we were successful.

The courage Cam displayed to try things he had never done before was inspiring. I can remember specific instances when he said yes to a big project or brought in something that he had created or done. Many times, I was simply speechless and in awe.

Cam also made sure that everyone was always taken care of. While he showed gratitude himself, he also wanted others to experience gratitude through his own service. And while this might sound like a father gushing about his son, it's not. It's a CEO talking about an employee. He was also one of my greatest teachers. He taught me how to genuinely love and care for people. He helped me remember what it felt like to be young and energized and to see everything as new and exciting.

Cam introduced the employee appreciation of the year award called, "The Angler." We now call it the CAM Award in his honor.

CAM'S COURAGEOUS FIGHT

Beginning sometime in 2007, Cam wasn't able to eat much. His work ethic and attitude hadn't changed, but we noticed that he was looking feeble. When he began losing more weight, we knew something was wrong, so we started seeing physicians and specialists. His condition progressively worsened to the point where he could hardly eat anything.

We eventually learned that his life was in serious danger. With tears streaming down his face, the doctor said that he had found a tumor growing underneath Cam's esophagus. Finding a tumor at this point was very serious, he told us. I can't remember his exact words, but I had known this doctor for nearly 20 years, and he is not a man who cries very often, if at all. When he showed this much emotion, I knew something was terribly wrong.

Cam underwent an ultrasound endoscopy to scan through his stomach. We discovered that the cancer had spread through the entire stomach lining—the tumor had been found at the spot where the lining had become the weakest. The doctor who performed the endoscopy told us, "He has zero chance of survival. We give him less than two weeks to live." That was in the middle of August 2007.

From that point on, Cam was left to our family's care. There was no protocol for this rare gastric cancer, as it typically occurs in men around the age of 72 who are just sent home to die. We knew of one surgeon who agreed to operate about a week later. We hoped that somehow, he'd discover that the other two doctors had been wrong.

It was scheduled to be an eight- to nine-hour surgery. However, within 45 minutes, the surgeon came out of the operating room, shaken. He told us that the cancer was everywhere. It had metastasized through all of Cam's internal organs.

Everyone assumed that Cam was going to die fairly soon thereafter—but Cam had other plans. He had shown his sense of fearlessness throughout his entire life—and he did the same, even more so, during the last six months of it. He never complained about his circumstances; in fact, he was quiet the first couple weeks. We found a doctor who also practiced alternative medicine in her own clinic with miraculous success. The day after her first consultation she invited Cam into her care. She took care of him tirelessly—sometimes well into the night—using IV therapy to restore his health and destroy the cancer. Cam strengthened and was even able to do a little bit of work on his laptop. From that moment, I accompanied him to this wonderful doctor, whose clinic was 75 minutes away, every single day. At night his mother and sometimes his siblings would care for him so I could sleep a bit.

I did not physically go into Fishbowl once over the next six months. I stayed connected through my computer and my cell phone, taking care of financials, making decisions, conducting meetings, and organizing things remotely while sitting next to Cam.

Our entire family made the decision to do everything we could to fight the odds. We expected a miracle, and had people around us praying for one. Cam suffered from pneumonia several times; he'd have to go to the hospital because his temperature was 106 or 107, and his heart rate would occasionally race to 170 or 180. These are things that people don't survive; yet they were nearly everyday occurrences for Cam. He persevered, fought, never doubted, and was so enormously courageous—every moment of every day.

The only thing Cam asked for was back rubs. His lower back was agonizingly sore because he'd lost all of his muscle. He would let us know he needed a back rub by wiggling his feet; anyone who was with him would rub his feet to ease his pain.

Toward the end, he lost the ability to do more and more things, but he would do anything and everything he could. Cam never backed down from his hope of survival, even on the day when he couldn't breathe anymore. They had to insert a ventilator and tape his mouth closed. Then they had to place a drainage tube in his nose for the blood that would build up in his stomach. He was also put on dialysis because his kidneys had shut down. With all of the artificial mechanisms keeping him alive, he was fairly listless and didn't move much. His eyes would stay open, but he would stare off into the distance. When we spoke to him, he would acknowledge us with a slight eye movement.

I recall, two days before he passed, that I leaned down to Cam and just said, "Cam, is there anything you want to say or anything you want us to do?" It was obvious what was happening, but we'd already resolved that we would never ever think or speak of anything but a miracle. We'd never even contemplated Cam's dying.

When I said this to Cam, he must have used all of the energy that he had to stare at me and give me a frown that said, "How dare you give up now, Dad!" I quickly backed away from asking him more questions and continued to pray for a miracle—right up to the last moment.

Eventually, the dialysis machine stopped because there was not enough pressure to keep it going. We didn't know what was happening; no one was telling us anything, so we had to ask about everything. So I asked the nurse, "What does this mean?"

She said, "They usually just last up to an hour."

It was two o'clock in the morning, so we figured we had until about 3:00 AM. I asked her what would happen and she said that the heart would pick up speed, and then drop dramatically. And then he would pass.

I don't know how many nights we'd gone without sleep, because we'd had to watch him so closely for the last several weeks as we did everything we could to help him. But now every member of Cam's family was there—surrounding him, hugging him, trying to stay awake or sleeping on the floor. When the dialysis machine stopped, we all hung on to him . . . but 3:00 came, and then 4:00, and then 5:00, and his heart was still beating at a normal pace. I kept waiting for it to start to go up, even as the nurses popped their heads in with a look on their faces that said, "He's still alive?!" But they didn't know Cam.

His heart rate started to go down at about 5:00, but it immediately came back up, and we thought, "Here's the miracle." We believe that our Creator can cause a miracle to occur at any time, so in spite of everything, we still believed Cam could be healed. But it was not to be—this was Cam's time to leave.

At about 7:00 AM, Cam's heart rate finally accelerated as the nurse had described—four hours after anyone in that condition is supposed to survive. My perception was that he wasn't in pain, and that he had already left his body, even though he hadn't yet died. After picking up speed, his heart began to slow. Then, according to the heart monitor printout I took home with me, he gave us a tremendous last heartbeat at 7:19:55.

CAM'S COURAGE INSPIRES FISHBOWL

Cam had a lion's heart, a brave heart. We called him "Iron Williams" after the movie *Iron Will*—he simply had a heart that was full of goodness and love in life, one that was difficult to stop, even in the face of death. Because of Cam, I believe we all have the capacity to discover our own brave heart.

His funeral was a beautiful experience. We celebrated Cam's life, even though we were all in shock. Each person goes through their own type of grieving experience. I believe his mother suffered in different ways than I did; I believe his sisters and brother suffered uniquely depending on how old they were, how close they were to him, and how they had served him. All of them had served him to the best of their capacity, and had given all they could. His younger sisters even moved back into our home and many nights were up with him or just around him while he was there. When I would bring him home late at night, his mother and siblings would take over so I could get a little rest.

Part of his great legacy, and one of the most important leadership lessons that he taught me, is that I could care for everything at Fishbowl the way he had. Most people think that when you hire your family member, you treat them differently. Today's leadership books generally advise against treating your family member employees as special. But why not look at it from a different perspective—and treat *everyone* as special? Instead of lowering the bar, consider raising it. I also discovered how tenderly we treat another human being when they have a serious illness. Why does something traumatic or dramatic have to occur to bring out the best in us? Why can't we skip "the stuff" and simply care for one another?

Cam left his family with a tremendous legacy that will continue to burn in our hearts forever. But Cam also touched the hearts of every Fishbowler. Through both of his families, his great legacy and example of courage continues to radiate to all humankind.

Cam's illness and passing was a very difficult experience for our family to endure—as well as for the Fishbowl employees who knew and worked with Cam. Yet they all stepped forward, carried the ball, and displayed tremendous commitment and loyalty. They all believed in Cam, too—that he would survive. I have deep gratitude for all those who worked at Fishbowl through those six months— whose support, both professional and emotional, allowed me to care for my son.

Despite the hardship of Cam's disease, Fishbowl continued to operate in a great way. And as crazy as it may sound, those last six months of his life were some of the best for the company up to that point. Some wonderful things happened during that time, and I believe that Cam's influence made them happen.

Cam knew how to rally people together. Because our employees knew Cam was fighting for all he had, he inspired them to go above and beyond, too. They exhibited an incredible ethic and achieved unbelievable things while I was out. Everyone upped their game and displayed the 7 Non-Negotiables in every way they could—and in ways I could never imagine. They made it possible for me to serve my son and be with my family throughout that horrendous experience. I was never judged negatively for not being there—including by the majority shareholder, who was the first to try and contribute personal funds for the cost of the alternative medicine Cam received, which insurance didn't cover.

Cam's oldest sister, Amber, led the charge in planning and executing the fund-raisers that provided much of the money we needed for Cam's treatments. This feat was another example of how Cam's siblings showed him great respect, love, loyalty, and courage—all while letting him know that he wasn't fighting his battle alone. They were out working into the night and many times through the day to raise money and awareness for this rare type of cancer.

The Courage to Live for Other People

We've all heard the question countless times throughout our lives: What would we do differently if we knew we only had one day left? How would we treat someone close to us if we knew we were going to lose them? It's not necessarily a pleasant thought, but I think it's one we should consider every day. It's a difficult practice to incorporate on a daily basis, but that makes the response all the more rewarding. And deep down, we all know the answer: We would do anything for that person.

Most of us remember to do this for their families, but overlook an important fact: We also spend 40-plus hours a week with our colleagues. We rarely think about bringing that spirit of care into the workplace—but we *should*. Remember: You may never know what another human being is going through, but we can still relate to them, due to the simple fact that they're a fellow human being.

One of this book's underlying messages is that all of us—whatever our organization or field, and whether we realize it or not—are in the people business. We need to remember that our relationships with our coworkers far outlast the work experience itself. The way we display the 7 Non-Negotiables will far outlast the projects we completed or the money we made. Remembering we are in the people business is where the "gold is in them thar hills!"

Because we at Fishbowl live the claim that we're in the people business, we invite other companies, entities, groups, families, to do as we do: to clearly show your people that they are valued as humans, not just as resources; that people are the most important part of any company. Their welfare—their ability to grow and be fulfilled and happy—is what we strive for at Fishbowl. We want all of our employees to have the opportunity to improve their self-esteem and self-worth, and to expand their competency and capacity. As this occurs in their work roles, it will cascade into all their other life roles, and it helps our people to become better spouses, parents, siblings, sons, daughters, community and church contributors, and flat-out better human beings. They are happier, healthier, and gain the extra capacity to then serve others.

These are the kinds of things that should *always be improving*. If we take care of our people at Fishbowl, we know that the natural outcome is that we'll be okay as a company. We talk about this a lot at our organization; it's truly something all leaders should think about. When they consider how to address matters with their employees, they should adopt the same paradigm as we have: that they are in the people business. People are not just resources to be used, abused, and cycled through; our goal is to have people stay on our team for as long as possible. They'll do their work if they're happy and fulfilled.

When people know that they and their families are cared for, as Fishbowlers do, their self-worth and self-confidence will grow by leaps and bounds. The potential locked within them simply requires a healthy and forgiving environment that grants them the space to try, stretch, jump, and do things they've never attempted before.

The Courage to Succeed—and to Fail

Cam personified this kind of trailblazer. He did and tried things that people before him had never done or tried in a whole slew of areas. This is the kind of spirit we try to keep alive at Fishbowl, by allowing our people to grow, take risks, and develop their own courage.

We look for this spirit in the people we hire. When a person comes to me with a desire to work at Fishbowl, I don't care what their résumé says, or how they look. One of our best employees came directly in to the Bowl from an oil rig. He was a bit of a roughneck at first, but he turned out to be one of the most loyal, courageous employees Fishbowl has ever known. Another came from managing the assembly of playground equipment; he is now one of our most esteemed leaders. Yet another was moving furniture in our office complex; he is now a top-tier trainer in our products and services. A fourth was an 18-year-old woman who became a support/training team leader of people older than her. All of them had something in common: They were good people who had greatness within. A different leader or investor might have looked at them and thought, "We can't hire these people. They have no experience in this kind of environment, and probably won't have a clue what they're doing."

But Fishbowl is different—we embrace this diversity. The fact that they're pretty odd in unique ways is what makes them so incredible. I believe that it was our job to give these individuals, who never had an opportunity to shine before, the chance to do so with us—and they've proven me right. They have all risen to the occasion at Fishbowl. Because we expected it of them, there was no option for anything but success.

It was a lot like what we endured with Cam. We never spoke of anything but a full recovery, and believed right up to his last heartbeat that there was a chance for a miracle. We used this same approach to turn Fishbowl around, and it's the same outlook we have today: Never think of anything but success. Are there tough moments? Certainly. But they compel us to take a step forward rather than back down. When most companies were shutting down or standing still in 2009 and 2010, we turned everything on. That put us in the position we are in today and propelled us ahead of everyone else.

It all comes from *courage*, one of our 7 Non-Negotiables, and the way it couples with the others because it is so powerful. Let me show you this in how I experience the Non-Negotiables we've explored so far with new hires. I have *respect* from the start for people who apply to work at Fishbowl or who are recommended for work here. There is always something about them, whether it was their characteristics or something they said or did, or the way they served someone. Whatever it is, it quickly makes me *believe* in them. I don't care what they've done or what their schooling or previous jobs have been; once they start and I see that respect and desire to give their best, I give them my full *trust*. It's pretty hard to lose my trust, in fact. You have to do something over and over and over again for me to finally give up and stop trusting you. I never stop believing!

I also strive to be completely *loyal* to people. I'm not perfect, but every day I try to be better. My loyalty arises from respecting, trusting, and believing in them. And part of showing your loyalty to someone means giving them room to err. If you give them a rope, you don't tie it around their neck and yank them back when they start to stumble and make a mistake. Rather, it's there for them to hold on to. You make a *commitment* to help people feel empowered, make a mistake, and Fail Up. We've seen time and time again at Fishbowl that when people are permitted to Fail Up, they respond incredibly well. Yes, they've failed in the past; but they just need a chance to be lifted up after they've stumbled. And once they do so, they become even stronger. They're able to achieve things that were even more difficult than they thought before they failed.

There's also power in committing to your team and your partners. They are the ones who will rally around the injured and help them get back up. Teams and partners have the courage to close ranks to protect those who are injured and take over their responsibilities until everyone is back on their feet and 100 percent again.

Write down the most important lessons you learned from the Courage Non-Negotiable and how you can apply it in your life.

1. _____
2. _____
3. _____
4. _____
5. _____
6. _____
7. _____

SUPPLEMENTAL MATERIALS AND EXERCISES TO DEVELOP YOUR OWN NON-NEGOTIABLES AND DEFINING ATTRIBUTES

The Attributes of Courage

1. Courage is the ability to remain true to the Non-Negotiables in the face of challenges.

2. Never back down from a challenge; find the strength to soar.

3. Face challenges alongside your teammates and push through them together.

4. Do what you know must be done at all times, whether you want to do it and especially if you do not. Accept all responsibilities assigned to you, whether you are ready for them or not.

5. Realize that we will face tasks each day that are not always pleasant, but accept that our actions are for the best. Always do what is right.

6. Have the courage to stand alone for something that is right, and humbly admit when you are wrong.

7. Move forward with your best effort, even when there isn't yet enough data to guarantee your choices will lead to the best solution.

COMPLETE THE FOLLOWING EXERCISES AND RETURN TO THIS SECTION TO ADD YOUR OWN NON-NEGOTIABLE AND DEFINING ATTRIBUTES

Enter your Non-Negotiable Value_____

1. _____
2. _____
3. _____
4. _____
5. _____
6. _____
7. _____

You gain strength, courage and confidence by every experience in which you really stop to look fear in the face. You are able to say to yourself, "I lived through this horror. I can take the next thing that comes along." You must do the thing you think you cannot do.

—*Eleanor Roosevelt*

True courage is not simply doing something difficult or that you are afraid to do, or facing fear or pain. Most working definitions of courage refer to truth, correctness, or doing what is right. For example: "doing what is right in the face of opposition" or "saying what is true regardless of the consequences." Being in the right is what gives us the motivation we need to be courageous.

A good example is Galileo, the inventor of the telescope, who used it to help prove the earth is part of the solar system and not the center of the universe. Sharing this truth got him into a lot of trouble with the Church, which imprisoned him for opposing the current dogma.

A collective example of courage that directly affects us all is our own courageous mother. Bringing a life into this world is a beautiful miracle; it is also a terrifying and potentially life-threatening endeavor. Even in a world of modern medicine, giving birth puts the mother's health and life at risk. Her courage to give birth comes from her love for that life that could be, which sustains her through every pain and inconvenience.

Courage that comes from truth is self-sustaining. Most people are more courageous than they think. Not doing something hard does not necessarily mean you are not courageous. However, if you know something is true, but you behave in an opposite manner, that is when you are not exercising courage.

BUILDING COURAGE FOR INDIVIDUALS

This exercise in courage is designed to build on small, incremental successes until things that once seemed impossible are now easy. The goal is to bring the things you know to be true, your true self, and your behavior into alignment.

Positive Affirmation and True Courage Orientation

1. The first step is to rediscover what you know to be true. Pick one role or area of your life, like your occupation, family relationships, or spirituality.

2. List a few things in that role or area in which you believe that you have conviction, that you know to be true or right.

3. Circle the ones toward which you feel you always demonstrate true courage (e.g., you stand up for them, though sometimes it is difficult).

4. Doing this will help renew your strength by reminding you of all the areas in life that you have conviction because truth gives us energy.

Truth in All Areas of Your Life

1. List a few things you know to be true in each of the areas or roles of your life (i.e., where you spend a regular amount of time each week—work, home, with friends, church, etc.).

2. This time, identify one thing in each area that you know is true or right where you sometimes or rarely show courage (i.e., you know it's true but you still behave otherwise).

3. Of all the ones you have circled, choose the one that seems easiest to overcome.

4. Identify the opposition or consequences that keep you from demonstrating courage.

5. Create a plan to help yourself change this dynamic. Have a friend help you do it, or take a small step first, so the remaining distance becomes a little easier. Then follow through with your plan.

Extra Credit: Courage in All Areas of Your Life

1. Once you have conquered your easiest thing, find the next easiest thing to work on.

2. Create a plan and follow through.

3. As you do this, you will become stronger with each small step and each small success until things that once seemed impossible seem surprisingly doable.

TEAM RETROSPECTIVE ON COURAGE

If you are looking to develop courage in a group setting, it can be beneficial to start with a group with whom you share similar convictions, like your family or coworkers. Using the previous exercise as a guide for your group, discuss, discover, and write down a few truths that you all believe and share collectively. Depending on the dynamic of your group, you may want to take turns telling your favorite story relating to each. Next, have each person recommend one way, or have the entire group decide on one way in which the group's collective behavior could be more consistent with a truth that they all have. Last, make a plan that all can participate in to collectively demonstrate more courage and bring everyone into alignment. And remember, as Ernest Hemingway said, "Courage is grace under pressure."

7

GRATITUDE

REFLECT on the Attributes of the Non-Negotiable to Develop Your Soft Traits

LEARN from the Failing Up Chronicles and Create Your Hard Results

DISCOVER Opportunities Earned

No one cares how much you know, until they know how much you care.
—Theodore Roosevelt

The Fishbowl Way: We polish everyone and everything around us until it shines.

REFLECTING ON THE ATTRIBUTES OF
THE NON-NEGOTIABLE

Gratitude is the reward of the Non-Negotiables because it is the one that ultimately brings us the most joy. At Fishbowl, we feel genuine gratitude when we see the 7 Non-Negotiables reflected in others. To complete the Retrospectives, I'll share a few stories of how the 7 Non-Negotiables inspired others who knew Cam. His spirit and legacy continue to produce extraordinary outcomes for us all. I am a better man and leader thanks to the life and legacy of my son, Cam.

Our employees often express gratitude that we placed them in positions that test and grow their skills. We believe in them. That is how we build star performers. We call them athletes. Our Fishbowl athletes have a fire in the belly so bright that it shines through in their countenance. I believe we all have an innate passion to do good things with our lives. We want to add value. Most people are basically honest and hardworking. There is an athlete in us all.

You notice I didn't say anything about their résumé or achievements. We bring people onto the Fishbowl team based upon their potential to learn and their willingness to develop with the team.

At Fishbowl, we often refer to this quote that was included in a dedication from Theodore Roosevelt:

> It's not the critic who counts; not the man who points out how the strong man stumbles, or when the doer of deeds could have done them better. The credit belongs to the man who is actually in the arena, whose face is marred by dust and sweat and blood; who strives valiantly; who errs, who comes short again and again, because there is no effort without error and shortcoming, but who does actually strive to do the deeds; who knows great enthusiasms, the great devotions; who spends himself in a worthy cause; who at the best knows in the end the triumph of high achievement, and who at the worst, if he fails, at least fails while daring greatly. . . .

Our secret sauce for keeping gratitude alive in the Bowl is that we trust that people are doing the best they can each day. All we ask is that they get into the arena and do their best. No treading water or sitting on the bench allowed on our team. Everyone gets to play on Team Fishbowl.

I would rather work with a committed junior athlete who is honest, hardworking, and teachable over a seasoned candidate with a spotless résumé. At Fishbowl, we do our best to teach our employees the correct principles that are included in this book and then allow them to govern themselves. If they are truly athletes with open and willing minds, they can become great and their output can be extraordinary.

Fishbowl's expectation of an athlete is that they can play multiple positions—that is, work in multiple departments and in multiple places within each department. We have had Fishbowl athletes work in virtually every role the company has, simply because they had the desire, competency, and capacity to work anywhere as long as they are challenged, rewarded fairly, and can maintain a good work-life balance. We realize that work is just one of the roles such athletes have in their lives, certainly not the highest on their list of importance.

We make sure our athletes are continually being conditioned through cross-pollination with others in the company. We also accept that sometimes even a great athlete can drop the ball. That's okay; we give our employees the ball again and again. We trust and believe in our people and demonstrate this trust by giving them new challenges and opportunities.

Dare to be surprised by those who appear average on the outside. Each person has extraordinary gifts and talents within them. They need a leader who believes, trusts, and respects them, one who will be committed to allowing this greatness to emerge. Begin giving them this trust the moment they start working, and then allow them to surprise themselves with what they can do, all because a leader believes in them.

THE STORY OF THE CAMSTRONG BRACELET

When people at Fishbowl serve beyond themselves and expect nothing in return, they are given a Camstrong bracelet. Our bracelets remind us that we are a band of brothers and sisters who never give in or give up and do our best to work with a spirit of open collaboration. As we embrace this journey together, we move forward in a spirit of cooperation and gratitude.

Cam accomplished great things in his lifetime, and those who supported him during his illness wore a blue bracelet created by his siblings to signify strength, hope, and belief.

Cam's siblings, Lindsey and Tanner, also designed an orange bracelet to help participants in the CAM Center to carry on Cam's legacy and to inspire Courage Above Mountains moments in others. The orange bracelet includes the words "Camstrong: Living and Learning."

Here are several highlights from individuals who knew and worked with Cam who have found their paths in life and earned their Camstrong bracelets by experiencing their own Courage Above Mountains moments. Additional information about the CAM Center is available at http://thecamfoundation.org.

NATE CHECKETTS'S COURAGE ABOVE MOUNTAINS MOMENT

A young man who served as a missionary with Cam in Italy was inspired by Cam's unquenchable spirit and moved by his battle with cancer. When he visited a shrine at the top of Mount Koressos where tradition says Mary, the mother of Jesus, spent her final years, he decided to honor Cam's memory by placing a CAM bracelet on a sacred prayer wall.

JAMESON KING'S COURAGE ABOVE MOUNTAINS MOMENT

A friend of Cam's was training for the World Championship Triathlon when he learned of Cam's plight with cancer. He wanted so badly to win for Cam, but many things went wrong during his qualifying race that it became torture just to keep moving forward. However, he kept going to honor Cam's struggle, and he made it to the end. He didn't win the race, but he won deep self-respect and peace.

My Personal Courage Above Mountains Moment Came As I Hiked the Canyon de Chelly

My personal Camstrong moment came when I placed Cam's bracelet at Canyon de Chelly in the Navajo Nation. It was time for me to get back in the arena and create an ongoing legacy that both Cam and my family could be proud of. I was ready to rededicate myself to create something worthwhile in service to others through the CAM Foundation. I also began helping others through my weekly *Forbes* articles, which ultimately led to writing this book. The bracelet remained high on that mountaintop for six months. The weather conditions are strong in this area. I mentioned once to our grant team that Cam didn't like camping or sleeping outdoors. In the summer of 2012, on one of their routine student visits, they retrieved the bracelet and surprised me by returning it to me and giving me pictures showing that the bracelet had survived the winter, spring, and fall. I still wear the bracelet today, along with the orange bracelet as a constant reminder that all things are possible and miracles do occur every day.

ERIC PEARSON'S COURAGE ABOVE MOUNTAINS MOMENT

Fishbowl's lawyer, Eric Pearson, made the arduous climb to the top of Mount Kilimanjaro, reaching an elevation of 19,341 feet. It was the most difficult physical challenge of his life—and he has run 23 marathons. He left two Camstrong bracelets at certain peaks to encourage people to keep going and reward them for finishing the journey. By doing that, he also made sure that Cam would always be on top of the world.

RYAN LONG'S COURAGE ABOVE MOUNTAINS MOMENT

Fishbowler Ryan Long lived in the same apartment complex as Cam for a time. Cam created a familial atmosphere among the tenants and he did the same thing among the employees at Fishbowl when Ryan started working there. During a trip to China, Ryan left a Camstrong bracelet on the Great Wall of China as a symbol of Cam's enduring influence on the world.

The Courage Above Mountains Center

By Devin Thorpe,
Forbes *contributor, popular speaker,*
and author of **Your Mark on the World**

Fishbowl Champions of Social Good: Inspired By Tragedy, Fishbowl Leaders Walk Their Talk

When I walked into Fishbowl Inventory I immediately noticed something unusual for an office: happy people. The reception area features both a Ping-Pong table and a foosball table—each was occupied by employees enthusiastically engaged in play (despite the fact that the Ping-Pong players would obviously not be competing for slots on the Olympic Table Tennis team anytime soon).

I was interested in visiting Fishbowl, headed up by a former colleague and friend from the past and fellow *Forbes* contributor, David K. Williams, who has written about having a "no

(continued)

(continued)

exit strategy" and encouraging employees to stay with a company for the long haul, and what he calls "The 7 Non-Negotiables." Dave and Fishbowl President Mary Michelle Scott are iconoclasts who are reinventing the discipline of management.

As Mary gave me a tour of the office, we interrupted a game of hearts—a 3:00 PM ritual for the newly constituted development team, where the vice president of technology works as a coder. Playing a daily game, which each member of the team gets the chance to choose, serves as a formal part of the team-building process at Fishbowl.

As we continued our tour, Mary explained that she and Dave believe that "happy employees make happy products." They've adopted an agile development approach with a Fishbowl take: The central premise is the presumption that everyone is doing the best they can. This attitude encourages people to actually do their best while explicitly accepting that mistakes happen and respecting the effort that creates them.

It was clear from my interaction with employees that they actually believe this. Mary and Dave make a point of constantly reinforcing the theme that they believe in their team. They trust them. Mary says, "Dave and I never finish anything. We start it and then turn it over to the team because they make it better."

Many of their employees are young, recent graduates of Utah Valley University. While the school is a fine institution, even in the relatively small state of Utah, the University's only really remarkable feature is its size; its number of students makes it the largest school in the state. None of the employees was introduced as an Ivy League graduate. Yet the company is growing dramatically and is profitable. Fishbowl is getting the most from its employees.

My primary interest in visiting Fishbowl was to learn about their Courage Above Mountains Foundation—the CAM Foundation—named for Dave's late son, Cameron, who was one of Fishbowl's earliest employees. Cameron, sick for 18

months, was belatedly diagnosed with gastrointestinal cancer, such a rare diagnosis in someone his age that it had not
been remotely considered until its latest stages. While doctors
recommended hospice when the diagnosis was made, his religious Mormon family chose instead to fight for life. Combing
faith and prayers with every available treatment, they extended
Cameron's life for six months.

After Cam passed away, it was Mary, before joining
Fishbowl, who challenged Dave to refocus his grief to do something to create a legacy in Cameron's name. Dave invited Mary
to join Fishbowl and to help him create and run the Courage
Above Mountains Foundation. Mary officially joined Fishbowl
in January 2011.

It is difficult to pin Dave and Mary down when asking them
to describe the mission of the CAM Foundation. They simply seek to do whatever they can to make the world a better
place, leveraging the available resources. It is a service-driven
organization that does not ask for external funding. The CAM
Center consists largely of surplus space in the Fishbowl offices.
Recently, the company, through the Foundation, donated 22
computers to the Navajo Nation. Neither Mary or Dave asked
the team to do it, but one day Mary discovered that the company engineers were using their daily game time to rehabilitate
the old computers, cleaning the hard drives and getting them
back into peak shape to be given away.

Dave and Mary, along with Training VP John Erickson,
recently wrote about how devastating fear can be in an office.
No one at Fishbowl is afraid. Rehabbing old computers for
donation might have been viewed in some companies as a dis-
traction (or worse), but at Fishbowl no permission was needed
and only praise was given.

Dave confirmed his view that doing service while on the
clock inspires employees. "It makes them better people; better
people do better work."

(*continued*)

(*continued*)

When I arrived at Fishbowl, I was officially greeted by one of the most genuinely kind people I've ever met. Marilyn Bigney serves as the Fishbowl receptionist, but is nothing like any receptionist I've ever met. She is neither the twenty-something, clueless about what is going on, nor the militant middle-aged guard dog I've come to expect in the role.

Marilyn, it turns out, has a story. Laid off in 2009 and desperate for new opportunities in 2010, she enrolled in a free class made possible through a coordinated effort through the National Science Foundation grant program offered through Utah Valley University. There she received training, got to know some of the Fishbowl people, and ended up interviewing to become its receptionist, a job she now executes with the enthusiasm of a cheerleader combined with the polish of an international diplomat.

The CAM Foundation serves virtually anyone in the community who has a need. Many of the people helped at the CAM Center are young people trying desperately to master a technical skill like learning to use QuickBooks in order to get a decent job. Some are senior citizens who've been essentially defeated by technology. Dave takes pride in the fact that those seniors who have completed the training—which is often difficult for them—find their swagger and enthusiasm for life restored simply because they've caught up with the information age.

Fishbowl doesn't require employees to do service through the CAM Foundation. They get equal credit for being involved with Boy Scouts or any other community service. Dave notes, however, that many employees appreciate the opportunity to get involved through the CAM Foundation because it is convenient. Absent the CAM Foundation, many employees who are involved wouldn't be doing community service because they wouldn't know where or how to get involved.

Leaders often talk about the need to treat others with respect and kindness. I've never seen anyone walk the talk like Mary and Dave at Fishbowl.

Write down the most important lessons you learned from the Gratitude Non-Negotiable and how you can apply it in your life.

1. _____
2. _____
3. _____
4. _____
5. _____
6. _____
7. _____

SUPPLEMENTAL MATERIALS AND EXERCISES TO DEVELOP YOUR OWN NON-NEGOTIABLES AND DEFINING ATTRIBUTES

The Attributes of Gratitude

1. Seek opportunities to express kindness in word and deed.

2. Always keep in mind that a grateful heart is a strong heart. Gratitude is a medley of humility, grace, and delight in everyday life. It is appreciation for the gift of being able to work, learn, and create with one another.

3. Readily show appreciation and return others' kindness. Remember that while it's fine to over-thank, it's never okay to under-thank.

4. Communicate with people face to face whenever possible. Use their name and common courtesies. Remember that "please" and "thank you" can go a long way.

5. Take the time to express thanks, and continuously give your all in appreciation for the opportunities offered.

6. Have a genuine sentiment of appreciation for what others have done for you. Gratitude doesn't require grand gestures, just simple humility.

7. Spend energy focusing on what you have, rather than on what you don't.

**COMPLETE THE FOLLOWING EXERCISES AND
RETURN TO THIS SECTION TO ADD YOUR OWN
NON-NEGOTIABLE AND DEFINING ATTRIBUTES**

Enter your Non-Negotiable Value_____

1. _____
2. _____
3. _____
4. _____
5. _____
6. _____
7. _____

Gratitude is one of the easiest Non-Negotiables to demonstrate; it is also the easiest one to neglect. Often while we are in the middle of a project, the energy is high, and people are engaged and pushing toward the end. Then when it is over, we get so excited to move on to the next project that we forget to show gratitude for what just happened. It is just too easy to forget to be grateful.

Gratitude is an affirmation of goodness followed by an understanding and finally an acknowledgment of where that goodness comes from. One of the coolest things about gratitude is that by nature, when you are being grateful, you cannot be negative. When you are focused on positive things, you cannot focus on negative things.

ACTIVITY OVERVIEW

Studies show that there are multiple benefits of gratitude. One of the best results of being grateful is increased happiness, which leads to more productivity. If we spend time looking for moments to be grateful, we will be happier and more productive people.

The goal of this activity is to turn being grateful into a habit. This activity takes just a few minutes every day for three weeks. The best time of day to do this is in the morning. Every day, choose one of the following items to do. It doesn't matter if you do the same activity every time or switch back and forth between the two activities—the results will be the same.

1. Write down three things for which you are grateful.
2. Write and send a positive message of gratitude to somebody you know.

After three weeks you will begin to notice how grateful you are for the many people, things, situations, and experiences you encounter. Also, the process will have a major effect on your engagement, happiness, and productivity.

Respect:
Seek to understand others
before you seek to be understood.

Belief:
If you believe in yourself, you can
Fail Up and overcome anything.

Trust:
Trust is the foundation of healthy
relationships and it must be earned.

Loyalty:
Promises must be more than
words, even if they require sacrifice.

Commitment:
Hold nothing back and
work like this is your last job.

Courage:
Never back down from a challenge;
find the strength to soar.

Gratitude:
Seek opportunities to express
kindness in word and deed.

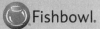

Fishbowl's 7 Non-Negotiables and Their Defining Attributes

8

TYING IT ALL TOGETHER

1. Applying Fishbowl's 7 Non-Negotiables to Achieve Hard Results
2. Seven Weeks to Hard Results
3. Remain Hungry for New Experiences and Opportunities to Learn
4. Great Companies Are Led by Missionaries, Not Mercenaries
5. Lead the Way to a New Organization

APPLYING FISHBOWL'S
7 NON-NEGOTIABLES TO ACHIEVE
HARD RESULTS

There are no secrets to success. It is the result of preparation, hard work and learning from failure.

—Colin L. Powell

Congratulations! You have completed your initial trek through the 7 Non-Negotiables. You might be wondering what comes next. Where do the Non-Negotiables lead?

To assist you in applying all that you have learned we have provided you with a list of work-related examples that demonstrate how a Soft Trait is tied to a Hard Result.

Using Fishbowl's own 7 Non-Negotiables as an example, we will show you how we've mapped our own Non-Negotiables into specific and deliverable results. You can use this format as a template to define your own non-negotiables. Then, the balance of this chapter will provide you with examples and stories of other companies and individuals who have led out in a similar fashion with their own defining Soft Traits, as well.

Let's get started.

1. Respect

Soft Trait:	Putting people before profit. Creating an environment where people govern themselves.
Hard Result:	A meaningful and inspiring work environment that people want to join and will seldom want to leave.
Example:	In this chapter, we share how growing too fast too soon can ultimately hurt an organization and how Lendio has made a conscious effort to put missionary motivations—the desire to help other entrepreneurs—above mercenary (profit-seeking) goals. The result has been award-winning growth and an exemplary corporate culture.

2. Belief

Soft Trait:	Believing in yourself and believing that your company can accomplish seemingly impossible goals.
Hard Result:	Sustainable long-term growth. Continuous record sales. Extreme innovation.
Example:	Steve Jobs is a remarkable example of a business leader who believed he and his company could accomplish great feats, no matter what others said. Could he have improved in a few areas? Of course. Fishbowl loves his intensity, purpose, and passion. Jobs encourages us all to "think and act different." Fishbowl believes in putting people before products and profit, and it has paid off significantly in the long run. We accomplished remarkable things at Fishbowl because we believed we could.

3. Trust

Soft Trait:	Believing the best in one another and having an unshakable faith in others, and focusing on earning the trust of others.
Hard Result:	Solid relationships with employees, communities, and vendors because these parties know they can rely on each other to behave with honesty and honor, even when sacrifice is required.
Example:	Partner organizations, such as Sharpe Concepts in New York City, create and market companion products for Fishbowl Inventory. They know their partnership with Fishbowl will provide them with reliable products and excellent customer service and training to support them in the advancement of their own organization.

4. Loyalty

Soft Trait:	Promises must always be kept. Individuals must believe in, and speak highly of, others, especially when they're not around.
Hard Result:	A company full of individuals who know they've got each other's back. No micromanaging because people are inherently motivated to do the right things without supervisors to watch what they do.

Example:	Fishbowl is a company that has no managers, in the traditional sense, to accomplish extraordinary results. Leaders can lead from the front, as opposed to driving from behind.

5. Commitment

Soft Trait:	Give your best effort when performing a task every day. Show up to work with a positive outlook and an energetic attitude.
Hard Result:	Productivity levels that exceed industry norms by vast margins.
Example:	Low employee turnover at Fishbowl. Exceptionally efficient operations, even with time set aside in the schedule for employees to exercise, offer community service, and play.

6. Courage

Soft Trait:	Persevere through any challenge and keep your eye on your end goal that supports the bigger organization.
Hard Result:	Extraordinary and unexpected results, even in competitive markets and difficult economic conditions.
Example:	In 2008 and 2009, Fishbowl doubled down on marketing investment while competitors retracted. Because of this, it was poised to achieve record growth when the economy turned around. In 2010, the company accomplished a 100 percent company buyback against all odds.

7. Gratitude

Soft Trait:	Always do your best to be kind and find ways to give back. Gratitude is a choice.
Hard Result:	Individuals who make time to help those in need within their own walls and within the community without being compelled.
Example:	Fishbowl's employees have conducted auctions to help each other during times of need. The employees organize the annual Day of Service to give back to their local community. The CAM Foundation is an effort that is entirely aligned to show gratitude to the legacy of my son, Cam, by paying it forward to communities and individuals.

At Fishbowl, we achieved extraordinary personal and professional results by living the Non-Negotiables in the reverse order. I invite you to follow these steps, as well.

Seven Weeks to Hard Results

The secret we discovered at Fishbowl to successfully applying the Non-Negotiables is to learn them in the following order: Respect, Belief, Trust, Loyalty, Commitment, Courage, and Gratitude.

We live them in the opposite order: We begin with *gratitude* and begin each day with thinking about everything we are grateful for. This places us in a positive state of mind and we can discover our inner *courage* to face challenges. It is easier to *commit* to what we are thankful for than for what we are not. *Loyalty* sometimes requires sacrifice. If you know what you stand for, you will also know what you are willing to sacrifice. Inner *trust* evolves naturally because you are living and working with integrity toward your own personal values and goals that you *believe* in and *respect* is born. This is a delicate path because life offers so many detours. We all get defocused and disoriented from time to time. There is no magic or quick fix. The results we are hoping for in life show up by simply spending more time than not on the path that works best for you.

Here is a simple exercise that we offer to get you started until you discover the unique ingredients that work for you.

Week 1: Gratitude

Write seven things you are grateful for that have nothing to do with you personally. Demonstrate your gratitude for at least one item on the list each day.

Week 2: Courage

Write seven things that cause you fear or stress. Work each day to remove the illusion of fear from at least one item on the list.

Week 3: Commitment

Write seven things that have taken root in you as a result of walking in gratitude and releasing fear. Commit to creating a new path at work based on these discoveries.

Week 4: Loyalty

Write seven things you are willing to sacrifice to show your loyalty to support and uplift others. Discover and implement at least one item each day.

Week 5: Trust

Write seven areas where your trust for yourself and others has developed and grown. Nurture each item one day at a time.

Week 6: Belief

Write seven new things you have found to believe in about yourself. Strive to increase your belief in at least one of these areas each day.

Week 7: Respect

Write the names of seven people you respect more than anyone else. Pattern your behaviors and attitudes after theirs to see what happens, focusing on one person each day.

WHAT CAN YOU EXPECT WHEN YOU REACH THE END OF WEEK 7?

You will likely lose the desire to judge others harshly and instead discover significant changes that need to occur within you. You will no longer need to demand credit for everything you do in order to demonstrate your value to others. This journey isn't about beating yourself up. It's about making small improvements day by day until you are surprised to find yourself standing far above where you used to be. We discovered in the Bowl that we focused less on changing others and organizations and lived less in judgment and more in discovery mode.

In the remaining sections of this chapter, we talk about several of these examples and the outcomes of Non-Negotiable decisions and actions in greater detail.

Two years ago, I had a chance to share a stage with Aaron Brown and Jeff Reeves, cofounders of Box Home Loans in Lindon, Utah. Fishbowl was being named twenty-fourth among the 2011 UV50 Top 30 Fastest Growing Companies, sponsored by Utah's *BusinessQ* magazine, but Box Home Loans had been named the top company, with a three-year growth rate of 1,811 percent.

Founded in 2006, and growing to 60 employees in five years, the company had achieved success that most can only dream of by doing mortgage lending only to high-credit-score customers. At their peak moment, they funded $101 million in loans in a single month.

I stepped up to congratulate Aaron, but what he said next took me by surprise: "Too much growth—too much money—coming at us too fast is not a blessing. In fact, it's a curse."

What?! He went on to explain: "Market conditions allowed us to grow really fast. But we're a company that thrives on providing a tremendous customer experience as much as a mortgage."

He went on to explain that Box Home Loans tries to provide the mutually exclusive experience of the best customer service coupled with the best possible price.

"Usually you go to Nordstrom to get excellent customer service, for example, but when you go to Nordstrom you don't expect to get a Walmart price," he said. "With controlled growth, we can do both. But with explosive growth—it can get us in trouble."

Box Home Loans has some characteristics that are unique to the mortgage industry, but there are aspects of what Aaron and his company are experiencing that apply to us all.

If explosive growth is a recipe for disaster, what's a business to do? In Box Home Loans' case, they made some key discoveries. They invested in Web analytics to better understand where their business was coming from, and which of these conduits they could most closely control. Some are beyond their control; when interest rates tick downward, loan applications flood through the door, but when they increase, business can dry up rapidly.

But they also discovered some mechanisms, such as their exposure on Zillow, which could be scaled up and down on the fly—even daily. "If we need more business, we price ourselves aggressively, and we show our rates on the tables we display on Zillow, and the business comes flooding," Aaron said. "But if we have too much inflow, we price less aggressively and we don't display the rates on the tables to slow the influx back down."

Another thing the company did was to increase its investment in technology, so that rate quote results, which typically take an agent 20 to 40 minutes to produce, can now be offered in a matter of seconds. "We're combining the best of high tech and 'high touch' to make our agents more efficient while giving our customers exactly what they need at the precise time that they need it," Aaron said.

The result: With only a few more employees, the company is now funding mortgages in 18 states, and funded $1 billion in new loans in 2012.

Traditionally, a loan officer might fund 5 to 10 loans in a month. A superstar might fund 15. But Box Home agents are each funding 60 to 70 loans every month while maintaining a Net Promoter Score (NPS) of 60 to 75 versus what Brown notes is an industry average of 18 to 20.

I saw Aaron again at the 2012 UV50 awards. His company was ranked fifteenth; ours was ranked twenty-third. I congratulated him again and asked, "How are you doing?"

"Great," he told me. "From 2010 to now, the difference in our business process has been night and day. We're perpetually looking at the ways to improve our process, but now it's getting to be really fun."

The company's profitability per employee is higher than ever. Its NPS scores are continually high. Aaron's growth rate in 2012: 165 percent. And his smile is twice as big as before.

Every company's situation is unique, but Brown's point is a good one: Be careful what you wish for. Too many customers too fast, without the proper controls in place to manage the process, could be the worst thing that could happen to a growing and successful company. When your company hits hyper-growth, be sure to take a page from the Box Home Loans playbook and put the right process in place to ensure your pace of growth is a blessing—not a curse.

Ask yourself: What is your own experience with managing explosive growth personally and professionally?

REMAIN HUNGRY FOR NEW EXPERIENCES AND OPPORTUNITIES TO LEARN

At Fishbowl we do our best to keep the company fresh. We fill the Bowl with innovative ideas. Last year we began building our first cloud-based products. Most engineering teams begin with a standard architectural design team. Our guys just dig in, learn, explore, and create. They are artisans who offer up their heart and soul in everything they do.

We have learned a great deal from Steve Jobs. We respect and admire him. The only area where we are perhaps a little different is that we love our people *more* than the products we build. Our people, not our products, carry on the Fishbowl legacy. I believe a great leader loves his people. It's miraculous what a team of fewer than 100 people has accomplished. They are not MIT-trained or elite, seasoned veterans. They come from all walks of life and represent a variety of beliefs and interests. Why does Fishbowl consistently win awards for outstanding products and services? Because we are just like our customers: hardworking human beings doing their best every day. We build practical products that help businesses across the country to thrive. I have also learned that many people with hard shells have soft hearts. I believe Jobs loved people in his way through the products he created.

And even though we differ on a few points, and most of our engineers would never part with their Android smartphones, there's a place in our hearts for Steve Jobs. The same fire he had to build the world's best products burns in our bellies, too. Both the Soft Traits and Hard Results come to life in the text of one of Apple's most famous ads and one of his most famous quotes:

> Here's to the crazy ones. The misfits. The rebels. The troublemakers. The round pegs in the square holes. The ones who see things differently.

They're not fond of rules, and they have no respect for the status quo. You can quote them, disagree with them, glorify, or vilify them. About the only thing you can't do is ignore them. Because they change things. They push the human race forward. And while some may see them as the crazy ones, we see genius. Because the people who are crazy enough to think they can change the world are the ones who do.

Think Different.

—Apple Computer

Stay hungry. Stay foolish.
—Steve Jobs, Stanford University commencement speech, 2005

Stay Simple—Love People and You'll Always Be Relevant.
—Fishbowl

Staying foolish ultimately means rediscovering a child's curiosity. It's your choice to allow others to convince you something cannot be done. You decide how you show up and engage in life, how you live your life, how you touch it, feel it, smell it, taste it, and experience it.

Blame, judgment, fatigue, worry, and fear—if you paint with these brushes, own it and accept accountability for it. But celebrate the fact that today, you can simply choose new brushes with which to create.

Staying FIT at Fishbowl

At Fishbowl, we do our best to adopt a healthy and energetic lifestyle through our internal organization called Fishbowl FIT. Every quarter we sponsor an athletic activity such as basketball, soccer, outdoor running, Frisbee—whatever motivates our employees and gets them moving. We keep it simple. There is no need to starve yourself. You should hunger for life, vitality, and

(continued)

(continued)

your dreams—not for food. You can review Fishbowl FIT and the free health programs we offer at www.7NNs.com. Also, consider reviewing the following points:

- What are your fitness goals?
- If you feel lethargic and cranky, it might be your diet—not your coworker.
- If you are a leader, lead the charge by serving as a fitness example for your team.
- Adopt a fellow employee who could use a hand up with their own fitness goals.

If you are challenged to remain on course, we suggest you consider following the wisdom and laws of Sir Isaac Newton. We refer to them often at Fishbowl.

CREATING AN ACTIVE AND INSPIRED WORK WEEK BASED ON NEWTON'S LAWS

1. *The First Law of Motion* is the Law of Inertia. It states that an object in motion will stay in motion unless acted upon by an outside force, and an object at rest will remain at rest unless acted on by an unbalanced force.

   What we can learn: You have inertia. You are either moving forward, backward, or remaining stagnant. The two latter options are not good, and they can be difficult to change. If you're moving away from your desired goal, you'll have to exert a great deal of energy to slow your retreat and stop moving backward. If you're not moving at all, it also takes a great deal of effort to overcome fear and motivate yourself to move forward.

   Inertia can work in your favor. If you're already moving forward, it's easier to make small corrections and adjust your speed instead of starting from a dead stop. We are the product of our thoughts, actions, and habits. You must first change your way of thinking if you want to do new things and form new habits.

2. *The Second Law of Motion* is the definition of force, expressed as force = mass × acceleration. A force is any power that influences an object to experience a change involving its speed, direction, and/or shape. Force can take multiple forms, such as pushing or pulling, and every force has both magnitude and direction, making it a vector quantity.

   What we can learn: You don't have to wait for outside forces to act upon you. You can push yourself to be better and accomplish more in virtually any area of your life. If you need help to make certain changes, you can ask for others' help to lift (or pull) you up, and then you can return the favor when called upon.

   When applying force in your life, be careful not to go overboard. If you apply too much force on an object, it will deform or break apart. Similarly, you must know your limits. Estimate how much effort is required to accomplish a goal and how much you can dedicate to it. Then pursue that goal over enough time to dilute the amount of stress so you don't have to take it all on at once.

3. *The Third Law of Motion* is the Law of Reciprocity. It states that forces come in equal and opposite pairs. In other words, "Every action has an equal and opposite reaction."

   What we can learn: Think about what you need to do to reach where you want to be. Identify three people who inspire you to reach higher. Talk to them and find out why they do what they do. Ask them for advice in making improvements in your life. Make sure your relationship with them is not purely one-sided by offering to help them as well.

Measure your changes over time by keeping a journal and writing down significant events in your journey. By seeing the reactions that occur as a result of your positive actions, you will be motivated to continue moving forward. Reaping what you sow is a natural law. Give your best effort each day and patiently watch the results unfold.

GREAT COMPANIES ARE LED BY MISSIONARIES, NOT MERCENARIES

Famous billionaire investor John Doerr, a partner at venture capital firm Kleiner Perkins Caufield & Byers, has often discussed the most important aspects of the world's greatest entrepreneurs and companies. In a 2000 interview, Doerr described the five characteristics that truly great ventures possess:

1. "The greatest companies are led by missionaries, not mercenaries."
2. "They have top-notch, passionate leadership."
3. "They operate in large, rapidly growing and under-served markets."
4. "They have reasonable levels of financing."
5. "And most importantly, they work with a sense of urgency."[1]

Doerr describes why missionary-led companies are so different from mercenary-led ones:

> Mercenaries are driven by paranoia; missionaries are driven by passion. . . . Mercenaries think opportunistically; missionaries think strategically. Mercenaries go for the sprint; missionaries go for the marathon. Mercenaries focus on their competitors and financial statements; missionaries focus on their customers and value statements. Mercenaries are bosses of wolf packs; missionaries are mentors or coaches of teams. Mercenaries worry about entitlements; missionaries are obsessed with making a contribution. Mercenaries are motivated by the lust for making money; missionaries, while recognizing the importance of money, are fundamentally driven by the desire to make meaning.[2]

Which kind of entrepreneur are you? At Fishbowl, we've worked to embody the missionary style of business and leadership for every step of our lives.

---

[1]Knowledge@Wharton, "Mercenaries vs. Missionaries: John Doerr Sees Two Kinds of Internet Entrepreneurs," Innovation and Entrepreneurship (blog), April 13, 2000, http://knowledge.wharton.upenn.edu/article.cfm?articleid=170.
[2]Ibid. Doerr also discusses the differences between missionary and mercenary management styles with entrepreneurs here: http://www.youtube.com/watch?v=wV2Md-Ujxgs.

Recently, I had the chance to discuss missionary versus mercenary leadership with the senior executive of another mission-driven company in our region, Burke Alder, vice president of marketing for Lendio. Lendio matches small businesses with lenders free of charge, greatly improving their likelihood of getting the financing they need to grow and prosper.

In the following paragraphs, Alder describes the differences in missionary versus mercenary management, and the way this differentiation has helped Lendio meet its business goals.

START WITH THE "WHY"

"In my mind, the concept of missionary leaders starts with the 'why' of the organization. Not the mission statement—which can be highly confusing—but the 'why' that speaks to the company's passion and vision for changing the world.

"TOMS Shoes is a great example: 'We are in the business to help change lives. For every pair of shoes purchased we give another pair to a child in need.' In Lendio's case, our passion is to fuel the American Dream. We want to help small businesses find the financing they need to grow, hire employees, and make a difference in the economy."

PEOPLE FIRST

"In a missionary culture, people matter. A missionary-focused company wants to make people's lives better. Knowing the 'why' of the company's purpose inspires and motivates people. The 'why' influences the reasons people want to work for a company. Companies that do this well appreciate the value of every person in their organization.

"In a mercenary culture it is the complete opposite. There is poor training and high turnover. People are motivated by and live in fear, rather than success. Employees are afraid to make a move; they're afraid a mistake could cost them their job."

FOCUS ON THE LONG TERM

"Missionary leadership is about building a company based on solving a problem that needs to be solved—a problem big enough that you're willing to focus on it for the very long term."

Alder notes that Evernote, the maker of productivity apps, is working to build a 100-year company. Fishbowl also is building a 100-year business. Alder continues: "Mercenary leadership, on the other hand, is short-sighted. Most conversations are about selling the company. It is looking for the short win—the build-to-flip model of creating a company. Employees also end up with a short-sighted view of the business, resulting in short-sighted decisions."

COLLABORATE

"A missionary-style company appreciates two-way feedback. Much of the company's motivation is to help people and to improve their lives. Furthermore, in a missionary culture you can make a mistake and still be okay.

"In a mercenary company, feedback moves only one way—from the top down. These companies don't promote collaboration well. They are poor at interdepartmental communications. They don't do a good job of prioritizing resources, and they are filled with people who are not truly engaged. At every level, these differences from missionary companies affect the way a mercenary business interacts with its customers. When its employees talk to customers, whether face to face or over the phone, they can't exemplify a company's passion, its mission, or its vision."

I agree completely with Burke Alder's assessment. Every priority he named is one that we strive to uphold in Fishbowl.

John Doerr famously noted one more incentive to build a missionary-focused company: They are ultimately the most profitable and financially successful. So when you consider the alternatives, which kind of entrepreneur will you be?

LEAD THE WAY TO A NEW ORGANIZATION

Companies need leaders, not managers. The organizations that truly thrive give *every* employee, from the top down, an opportunity to lead. But each employee is likewise responsible for shaping and creating his or her own future. It all starts by treating each person as "Me, Inc."—an organization of one within the larger organization.

What does that look like? We start with one of our 7 Non-Negotiables. We trust and then we empower. Far too many leaders claim to empower their people and then don't. The minute someone makes a mistake, they use the rope around their neck to pull them back. When people get yanked back like this, their natural reaction is to hunker down and become less instead of growing to become more.

Fishbowl's model of leadership is based on trusting people to make decisions and offer solutions without the threat of such tethers. As described in Chapter 2, we embrace a system of paired leadership, starting at the top of the company. My business partner, Fishbowl President Mary Michelle Scott, and I form a holistic, high-altitude view of what we want to achieve. Then we bring in the department Captains—of which there are three pairs, one per department—and involve them in what we're thinking of doing next. These leaders play a core role in the strategy's formation, and run the day-to-day deployment of the strategy that we've jointly created and set.

For instance, we might simply tell the Captains, "We think it's time to open up Canada, the UK, and South Africa." We then turn that big piece of meat over to them. They chew on our idea for a few days and usually come back with one of two responses: (1) they don't like it (which they generally couple with a counterproposal) or (2) they see multiple ways to go about achieving the goal.

The Captains don't "manage" every day. They have just one meeting per week to determine strategy. After we hand something off to the Captains, they hand it off to their teams, who in turn share it among the individuals who are deployed day to day to solve problems—and then the Captains get out of the way while resuming their own production roles, side by side with their teams.

Our approach makes the groups and leaders autonomous, but also interdependent. Team members are intelligent and creative, and all of their voices can be heard. Our team members usually come up with better answers than we could ever hope to achieve on our own. We then decide on the best idea, no matter who originates it; most of the time, we actually forget who brought the idea forward. Nobody worries about the glory because all will benefit as a team.

We learned these concepts of management and leadership by Failing Up, from the real-life stories told in our Captains' meetings. There's a fine line between management and leadership, but there's a massive difference as well, and our Captains seek to maintain the balance. Fish cannot swim through ice, so Fishbowl leaders keep our waters at the optimal temperature. We have one universal rule: Don't tap hard on the glass. This is the cause of so much upheaval in business today—because it startles the fish and some go belly up.

We have also learned that different divisions of an organization create their own cultures, schools of thought, and personalities. What motivates our sales department is different from what motivates and drives our development teams—and there is no one-size-fits-all solution. Small and agile groups thrive. They keep the water at Fishbowl filled with vitality and allow great things to grow every day. To foster this process, we knocked down all our walls, figuratively and literally, to create large areas where people can effectively collaborate and communicate. There are no isolated cubicles at Fishbowl.

At this point, our entire company is flat. With a flat hierarchy, everyone leads within their areas of stewardship and responsibility. Many will have excess capacity and offer to help another teammate, or they will even go to another department to see how they can help. This allows ideas to be cultivated and propagated, and keeps leaders accessible—right to the top.

While my door is always open, my policy is simple: "Don't come to me with a problem." In traditional settings, it is all too tempting for anyone to drop their problems in the lap of the leader or manager. By contrast, I tell my team members to keep me out of the situation *until* they're ready to come forward with the best solution or set of possible solutions. I also ask, "Did you take it to your teammates? What did they say?"

Rarely does anyone need to come to me after they've done all this. But even when they do, it is in a context of collaboration and sharing; they're not registering a complaint or asking me to solve their problem for them. Although there are some management components to this style of leadership, we try to keep from micromanaging. That only causes people to fear making a mistake and prevents them from being innovative.

Fishbowl didn't choose its Captains because of their educational degrees or technical backgrounds. We applied the 7 Non-Negotiables to find individuals with the right aptitude; and they, in turn, are using the 7 Non-Negotiables to find and guide the individuals on *their* teams.

For the past 22-plus years, I have lived within walking distance of LaVell Edwards Stadium, home to Brigham Young University's football team. Many great athletes have taken to that field and discovered the champions within themselves. Former Coach LaVell Edwards, one of the most extraordinary coaches of all time and member of the College Football Hall of Fame, teaches a lesson that we at Fishbowl hold so dear: success is in the preparation. When it comes time to play and score, those who have not sufficiently prepared may come up short.

The most important part of preparation is looking deep within yourself and discovering if you have the will to go the distance. The game of life comes with a variety of challenges. We've all heard the quote from *Hamlet*, "This above all: to thine own self be true." This is not about what you like or have a fondness for; rather, it poses the question: For what do you have the *will to go the distance*? What can you respect, believe and trust in, be loyal and committed to, and be courageous and grateful for?

Life is made up of countless questions. I have filled this book with an abundance of them and I urge you to keep a journal so that you can discover your own unique Non-Negotiables and your ultimate calling in life.

9

CREATING A LASTING LEGACY

You can't build a reputation on what you are going to do.

—Henry Ford

Think about your favorite author or writer and how his or her works most resonate with you. Now think about this: Have you considered that *you* are the author of your life—and that you can write yourself a good one?

At Fishbowl we have adopted the Agile methodology with Captains Kevin Batchelor and Heber Billings. Any software manager will tell you that one great developer is worth five good ones. I will not disagree with this statement as an axiom. However, this simply isn't our style at Fishbowl—because as I've emphasized throughout this book, we are in the *people business*. While we insist on building great software, we are much more interested in building great *people*. To reconcile this requires a good deal of patience and a commitment to a principle known as the Agile Prime Directive. It states:

> Regardless of what we discover, we understand and truly believe that everyone did the best job they could, given what they knew at the time, their skills and abilities, the resources available, and the situation at hand.
>
> —*Norm Kerth,* Project Retrospectives: A Handbook for Team Reviews

We have become fairly adept over the past several years at producing excellent products with rough talent. I think this evolution came from the notion that we at Fishbowl don't really enjoy working with genius prima donnas. We would rather work with our friends, even if they are still polishing their skills. At the same time, we need to consistently deliver high-quality software releases.

To do this, we rely on two important principles. First, we trust in the process of *incremental collaborative improvements;* and second, we focus on building close-knit teams who care more about *improving their contribution* than on developing individual strengths or eliminating weaknesses.

Our development teams live by this concept of making small, incremental improvements. We try to release our software often in order to quickly learn from our mistakes. The core concept of both the Agile Prime Directive and incremental improvements is the practice of holding *regular, formal retrospectives*. These gatherings are designed to provide a forum for analyzing a team's successes and failures, and implementing changes that will make improvements. Our development teams hold these meetings often; they put a lot of energy into making them a focal point of change. The retrospectives provide feedback that inform individuals and teams of various ways to make course corrections. We take them seriously and performing them is mandatory.

There are a few ground rules to retrospectives. First, as noted, they must be held regularly. It's tempting for a team to hold one retrospective and never repeat the process, since it's sometimes a painful (yet cathartic) one. Second, participants should assign an impartial moderator as host, to keep the meeting timely and on task. Ideally, the moderator is from a different team and can keep conversations from meandering so participants don't indulge in tangential rants.

Last, participants should create a time-boxed agenda and stick to it. They dedicate the most sensible amount of time to each retrospective activity they plan, and never let it run over. We normally divide our retrospectives into five sections:

1. Check-In
2. Data Collection
3. Data Analysis
4. Goal Setting
5. Rate the Retrospective

Our first step, *check-in*, serves as a mini-mixer. It's designed to make people feel comfortable, get them talking, and set the tone for the remainder of the meeting. We often play thinking games during the check-in, or ask get-to-know-you questions. Check-in should be *fun*—just as the retrospective should be a meeting that people look forward to. Sometimes this phase takes up most of the retrospective meeting; other times it only lasts a few minutes. The idea is to think about the people present and their reasons for holding the retrospective.

Once you have a general idea of why you're meeting, you can allot the other phases accordingly. For instance, if a fairly new team is performing a project, the check-in may be the most valuable part of the retrospective. Spending some time engaged in fun activities together may be enough to create meaningful improvement.

In the second phase, *data collection*, we gather qualitative data about how a project went. We take some time to remember each phase of a project, when it happened, and who was working on it. We call out key successes, horrendous failures, and offer any other observations needed, and write these items on whiteboards for all to refer to later. And while it can be a challenge, we try to come up with creative ways to get people to think about their failures *without* being cynical or negative. We do this by dreaming up elaborate games that make this part of the retrospective informative yet fun. There's one in particular where each team member is given a piece of dry spaghetti for each failure. After a few minutes of data collection we have tower-building contests to see who can make the tallest one from our failures. Make sure you set a time box for this phase and always end on time.

We actually spend a lot of time discussing project failures during the *data analysis* phase. We are careful to moderate these discussions closely, and we have rules that prevent one person from dominating the conversation. We also do our best to encourage comments from those who normally don't like to speak; remember, still waters run deep. When running retrospectives yourself, if you have several quiet people in the group, seat everyone in a circle and only allow each person to talk to the person on their right in turn. Discourage people from blaming individuals and encourage the team to accept faults as a group. It is important that team members have no fear during a retrospective and that there be no sacred cows. Again, follow your timebox rules.

In the fourth stage of a retrospective, we *set goals*. We like to create objectives that are easy to achieve but that also make a big difference in our processes and teams. Keep the goals fairly small, and post them in your workspace for all to see. As with most things, we like to turn goals into games—the more engaging, the better. People will remember the goals if you post big and even somewhat strange reminders of them throughout the office. For example, one of our development teams purchased a 1,000-piece Lego castle. For each unit test that was written, they attached one Lego to the castle set.

Make a group effort to *verbally commit* to your goals. Ask team members if they can commit to accomplishing a given goal by a particular date. Allow people to say no, if they truly feel they cannot. If not everyone agrees, retool your goal to be more achievable. A team's inability or lack of desire to work toward a certain goal might indicate a trust problem. The most important aspect of achieving goals is they boost people's confidence in their ability to *believe they can* accomplish a goal. At Fishbowl, we believe that lots of little achievements lead to a greater sense of success—more so than one huge goal that seems out of reach.

Last, we take a few minutes to *rate the retrospective*, and ask how we can make it better next time. This can be as simple as leaving comment cards for those inclined to make suggestions, or holding an informal discussion on the way out the door. Even retrospectives need retrospectives.

While the objective of a retrospective is to root out failures, its value lies in bringing about constructive changes in individuals, processes, and teams. To do this, team members must trust one another implicitly—not only as colleagues, but also as *friends*. We employ some simple social mechanisms to build friendships among teams. They are as old as human society and are simple to implement:

- Work together
- Eat together
- Play together

To fulfill the first objective, we custom-built an area for our development and support teams that allows them to sit in a comfortable and open shared space. We find that the ideal team size for just about any task is six to eight. Based on this size, each team shares a large custom-built office, well lit, with windows and *no cubicles*. The communal space provides natural accountability, encourages communication, and reinforces the social aspects of a team.

Each team is also self-sufficient and self-led. Allowing teams to operate almost autonomously creates an intrinsically motivating work environment.

We also believe that teams should eat together at least once a week. For some reason, people who often eat together trust one another. This is an ancient ritual; for thousands of years, human beings have developed bonds of friendship and commitment while sharing a meal. And not only should teams eat together; they should invite members of other departments to eat *with* them. For instance, our development team makes pancakes for the whole company once a week. We all sit and eat together as we discuss our development plans, make jokes, and show our progress. This ritual creates an environment of trust. It provides a venue to discuss our customers' concerns, and helps development, sales, and support learn one another's jargon and style. Additionally, the trainers invite product managers to lunch once a month. These events encourage giving, sharing, talking, and creativity.

Last, teams should get—and be encouraged to *use*—time to play together at work. This might sound a little crazy, but there are few activities that build as much friendship and trust as play. The collaboration that play develops can make a team more successful. Playing games together often leads teams to be more forgiving toward each other. It encourages teams to learn from one another—and, most important, it makes people happy. For the first three years of Fishbowl's existence, the development team played cards together every day at lunch. They played 700 games of Hearts and tracked every win and loss on a whiteboard in the hall. No matter how heated a debate about development got, they gathered around a table for lunch and played. This activity mended hurt feelings and rejuvenated relationships.

Companies can also use this game time to bring different departments together. Table games like foosball and Ping-Pong are great ways to gather support, sales, and development in the same place. You can also encourage and sponsor sports teams *outside* of work. If a support tech and a developer can become friends at work, they will solve customer problems faster. If a sales rep and a support tech trust each other, their post-sales handoff to customer service will be smoother.

CLOSING THOUGHTS
WHERE DO WE GROW FROM HERE?

What could we accomplish if we knew we could not fail?

—Eleanor Roosevelt

7 NON-NEGOTIABLES: RECAP OF THE LESSONS LEARNED

1. Devote your full attention to people when listening to them and defuse tension by putting time between the stimulus and your response. Doing this will build empathy and respect for others.

2. There is never a good reason to be unkind, especially in business. Business leaders need to reevaluate their business practices and eradicate outdated fear-based tactics. Focus on solving problems and believe in individuals' ability to learn from their mistakes.

3. Healthy organizations focus on the quality of relationships across their hierarchy. If employees feel safe providing input and talking with people in any area of responsibility, great ideas will flow and trust will be the norm.

4. You can come through the darkest moments of your life stronger if you have the right attitude and you don't give up. Loyalty is forged in adversity. We all get knocked down; what matters is that when we fall we discover a way to get back up. True leaders also help others get back up.

5. True leadership is selfless. When you make the commitment to put your team's needs above your own, you will find that together you can accomplish much more than you could have alone.

6. It's impossible to live life free of fear, but you can't let it dictate your actions. Even if you are in a battle you have little hope of winning, you can at least inspire others through your courageous example.

7. There are so many lives to bless, problems to solve, and people to uplift. Take a look around and be grateful for all the good you can do every day.

Write down the most important lessons you learned from the 7 Non-Negotiables and how you can apply them in your life.

1. _____

2. _____

3. _____

4. _____

5. _____

6. _____

7. _____

RECOGNIZING AND APPRECIATING THE MIRACULOUS MOMENTS IN BUSINESS

Our forefathers built this great country not for profit but for people. Likewise, the Fishbowl story does not end here, because we know that the bottom line is our people, not our profits.

People are continually evolving. I still trust my gut instincts over computer-generated analytics. I walk down the hall and see the countenance on our people's faces and know we have set a good course. Some of the best work you will ever perform as a leader is away from your desk and your computer. It's possible in small-to-medium-sized businesses to know everyone's name, to know their families and those closest to them. The fact that we have no exit strategy empowers us to effectively demonstrate to our teams the importance of making sure these behaviors are a part of our everyday dispositions. There are no short seasons at Fishbowl. This is our 100-year-and-beyond commitment.

By applying the 7 Non-Negotiables, we have discovered a deeper level of commitment and loyalty in business. When leaders teach the principles they want to show up in their organization, people will govern themselves according to what they learn. My business partner, Mary Michelle Scott, often points out that on the other side of failure is an opportunity. She helped us to see the potential within ourselves and our company. If we keep teaching our employees that and provide them with the necessary tools, time, and space to put it into practice, the miracles will emerge and the company will soar. People and life will consistently exceed expectations.

FULFILLING A PROMISE

So what comes next for Fishbowl, after we bought the company back, repaid the loan, remained debt free, and created the best inventory tracking software on the planet?

The answer is: We fulfill the promise we made to the people who went the distance. We asked these young people to trust us—to have faith that we could build an organization worthy of them. We honored our promise, and today 71 people share in the ownership of Fishbowl—and we're committed to future annual distributions. The employees of Fishbowl dug in, delivered, and served up a win in every way. They truly are champions, and they are all going to do such amazing things with their lives, for their families and the world. They are our legacy.

> You cannot lift another soul until you are standing on higher ground than he is.
> You cannot light a fire in another soul unless it is burning your own soul.
>
> —*Harold B. Lee, eleventh president of the Church of Jesus Christ of Latter-day Saints*

There is no perfect way to build a business. We respect all paths. We simply chose a road less traveled.

You have read about some of our extraordinary triumphs and tragedies. Why would an individual want to give their all to a company? Does an employee really want to work their guts out, only to see a few people at the top receive the reward? Why would an employee want to build innovative products and services that generate great revenue, just so the owners can sell the company and cash out? These are questions we asked ourselves on behalf of our employees. Creating an employee-owned company means that 71 people protect and preserve the Bowl and feel honored and respected for doing so.

I am writing the last chapter of this book just as those employees who have consistently demonstrated the Non-Negotiables for one year are coming in, one by one, to apply for ownership. Here are the questions we asked them:

- What is your dream for Fishbowl 100 years from now?
- Why is ownership important to you?
- How have you exhibited the 7 Non-Negotiables in working with employees in other departments?
- What is your personal vision statement?

What did we learn, as leaders, from these new owners? The majority of our employees asked that we not change or lose the culture as the company grows. They like working with one another. They believe in Fishbowl. They believe our company has integrity and that we stand by our word.

Many companies fail because they place all the responsibility on one or two people at the top. We are all human. If you really want to build a lasting company, build it with everyone. "TEAM" really does stand for "Together Everyone Achieves More." Surround yourself with good people. I never understood the need for CEO executive thought leadership groups, where CEOs connect with other CEOs to help build their companies. Why don't they just take seven or eight employees to lunch and seek to understand, build, and grow together?

For those courageous souls who are ready to take their companies to the next level, I encourage you to implement the principles I have discussed throughout this book. I have been amazed by the results, and I believe you will be, too.

Fishbowl has no ending, and there is no such thing as failing completely.

Every day is a new adventure and another opportunity to try again.

May all your Fail Ups be extraordinary!

And yes, I still love to FISH!

ABOUT THE AUTHOR

David K. Williams serves as chief executive officer of Fishbowl, the nation's leading provider of inventory management software for SMBs and asset tracking solution for large enterprises. Fishbowl Inventory is the No. 1 inventory management software add-on for QuickBooks® users, and is one of Intuit's original Gold Developer partners.

The company has achieved numerous awards for its continually fast revenue growth. Fishbowl grew 70 percent in 2011, the same year it achieved a 100-percent company buyback and added partner Mary Michelle Scott, who became president of Fishbowl. In addition to completing the buyback and becoming debt-free, David and Mary also created the Courage Above Mountains Center to serve as Fishbowl's corporate social responsibility outreach program. In addition to providing business incubation space and educational programs for small businesses in the Utah community, Courage Above Mountains provides learning, health, and enrichment services to underserved individuals in the United States and abroad.

The company serves as the catalyst for growth through business partnerships in the Fishbowl Partner Nation, Fishbowl Developer Network, and Fishbowl Referrer Program. David is a frequent speaker and author on business leadership topics and he writes for *Deseret News*, *Harvard Business Review*, and *Forbes*. He also brings a distinctive vision and passion to his position that empowers employees to accomplish more than they might think possible. This unique leadership skill is what transformed a small, struggling software development group into an industry leader in just a few years. Fishbowl has won dozens of awards for its impressive growth year after year from Inc. 500/5000, Inc. Hire Power, Deloitte, Global Red Herring, and Smart 25, as well as numerous Utah business awards.

David was honored as one of vSpring Capital's Top 100 Venture Capital Entrepreneurs in 2011 and 2012. He is a member of the Woodbury School of Business National Advisory Council at Utah Valley University, where he mentors business students and prepares young entrepreneurs to succeed in the business world and also serves on the Utah Valley Chamber of Commerce Executive Roundtable.

You can also read a Wikipedia article about David at en.wikipedia.org/wiki/David_K_Williams.

INDEX

Page numbers in *italics* indicate photographs

Your journey is just beginning. Let Fishbowl Inventory—the most popular inventory software for QuickBooks users—guide your business through the complexity of inventory management.

Call Fishbowl at 1-800-774-7085 and mention this book, *The 7 Non-Negotiables of Winning*, to get 15% off your purchase of any Fishbowl Inventory products, software training, or *The 7 Non-Negotiables of Winning* training.

Gain access to supplemental training services that accompany the book at www.7NNs.com.

Get *The 7 Non-Negotiables* of *Winning* online accelerated learning kit with your purchase of any Fishbowl Inventory product.

Contact Fishbowl President Mary Michelle Scott at mary.scott@fishbowlinventory.com for a list of training opportunities on the 7 Non-Negotiables.

For more information about Fishbowl, visit www.fishbowlinventory.com/.